Sustainable Dev Environments with Docker and Bash

Build a Stable and Maintainable Place to Code

David Bryant Copeland

For more information, visit https://devbox.computer and https://declare-ai.org.

Contents

Contents

Preface

Over the last four or five years, I've written several tech books, worked at a startup, and pursued many personal projects. Docker has allowed me to focus on the work and not on getting software re-installed for the 80th time just because Apple changed something.

I've refined how to use Docker for development, applying the same general principles to Ruby on Rails, NodeJS, CSS, and writing technical books. The consistency it brings, along with the value created by carefully writing the Bash scripts needed to glue it all together, has allowed me to focus, multi-task, and get things done.

A great example is this book itself. The toolchain[1] I use to write books requires a lot of tools, including some weird ones, like Graphviz, LaTeX, pandoc, Ruby, NodeJS, and Mermaid. Getting them installed on my Mac is difficult, so I put them all into Docker. I took a three month break from working on this book and got a new computer in that time. The first time I started up the book's development environment on my new computer—which only had Docker installed—everything just worked.

Another part of it is that I took the time to write decent Bash scripts to automate aspects of Docker. Docker was clearly not designed for an everyday developer to be typing its commands, but this is what Bash is for!

Docker and Bash aren't the most beloved or easy-to-use tools, and I will be pointing out their various issues in usability and intuitiveness as we go. But they are ubiquitous and, despite some rough edges, they both work, and work reliably.

Acknowledgments

I'd like to thank the Docker team, since they made a useful tool and created a great ecosystem. I will be throwing a lot of shade their way in this book, but it just means that Docker is worth criticizing. I'm glad that Docker is something I can complain about, instead of something no one has ever heard of.

I'd also like to thank whoever has worked on Bash over the years, particular whoever has continually made it backward compatible. When I find a Bash answer on Stack Overflow, it always works. ChatGPT is even right more than half the time!

I'd also like to thank the many tech reviewers who gave me great feedback on early versions of this book: Jason Garber, Reid Gillette, Sam Livingston-Gray, and Bradley Schaefer.

Change Log

- May 27, 2024
  - Address various typos
  - Fix code listing that omitted `source=$(pwd)` causing bind mounts to source code to not work

[1] https://www.naildrivin5.com/blog/2023/02/03/toolchain-for-building-programming-books.html

  - Updated NodeJS install instructions and adjust text to account for the changes
  - Move to NodeJS 22
- March 24, 2024 - Initial Release

1

Your Dev Environment Sucks

MacOS Bakersfield is our best version of macOS, yet. We've replaced the long-deprecated version of Ruby with nothing. You'll have to build Ruby yourselves, and you'll get to use our exciting new compiler flags that we haven't bothered to document. We've also managed to make sure that Homebrew now requires your iTunes password with every install. Only Apple has the courage to make this update to your computer without your consent. Oh, and one more thing: Your wiki is out of date.

—Craig Federighi

They say people don't quit their jobs—they quit their managers. I think developers often quit their dev environments. The hodgepodge of tools, libraries, scripts, and documentation required to actually build software is pretty important. So why does it seem to be broken all the time? In my almost 30 years writing professional software, I have not experienced a truly awesome dev environment. I bet you haven't, either. We're going to change that.

Dev environments suck because of a perfect storm of factors. Once you set one up, you rarely set it up again, so any instructions on how to do it are instantly obsolete. Hardware and software across even a small dev team is wildly inconsistent.

Operating system vendors and security teams force updates that break transitive dependencies. Any automation has to work in a degenerate environment where no other software has been installed, which makes it hard to write and change.

On top of all this, usually no one owns the dev environment. Each team typically has at most two experts: the developer that set it up initially and whoever was the most recent new hire.[1]

It doesn't have to be this way. We aren't woodworkers whose working environment is a physical space occupied by heavy machinery that can't be moved or replaced. A dev environment is a software system. We know this.

[1]And let's be honest, everyone else on the team is in a race to see if they can get promoted to management or hired at a competitor before IT refreshes their computer and they have to rebuild everything.

What You'll Learn

This book is going to show a way forward using Docker and Bash. That's right... Bash. But this isn't a blog post where I tell you what incantations to paste. You're going to learn how Docker works. You'll set up a dev environment by first running painfully verbose counter-intuitive Docker commands. This is how you'll learn what's going on. Then, you'll make it all better with well-written and nicely-crafted Bash scripts.

With just Docker and Bash you can automate just about any dev environment you can imagine[2].

Here is how this is going to go: We need a bit of theory to ground us in the problem we're solving and why the solution this book presents is the best, all things being equal. We'll learn what a dev environment is, and why the best implementation is automation of a virtualized environment. Our theory will end with an overview of Docker's terminology and behavior. You'll want to bookmark that chapter.

We'll then use Docker and Docker Compose to make a generalized dev environment for an example app. In addition to seeing Docker in action, we'll learn the right way to choose base images for use and the right way to install software in the images you will build. It's marginally more difficult than using Stack Overflow, but will produce far superior-and sustainable—results.

After that, we'll wrap up all those Docker commands with some general-purpose Bash scripts. But these will be no ordinary Bash scripts. They will provide *help on the command line*. They will be easy to use. They will even use some features of good software design so that someone other than the author can make sense of them.

What You Need

To use the tools we'll cover, you need a computer capable of running Docker. That means any recent Linux box, Apple computer, or a Windows-based PC that has Windows Subsystem for Linux 2 (WSL2). All of these platforms will contain Bash.

For completeness, I'm running Docker Desktop 4.20.1 and GNU Bash 5.1.4. Anything close to these versions will be fine.

[2]Except iPhone apps. For those you are stuck with Xcode, the App Store, and a 27% markup on an untestable payment processing experience you must maintain on behalf of customers you cannot contact. I'm very sorry if this is your life, and I hope your app is a hit.

A Note on Windows

If you are using a Windows PC, you really should use WSL2, which is free and easy to install. Like... so easy I couldn't believe it. Once you do that, and then install Docker, you *must* follow the post-install instructions[a] on Docker's website.

Your WSL setup will have you running Linux as a normal, non-root user, and by default, that type of user can't use Docker. The instructions at the link work - I did this using a Windows PC having not touched Windows at all in probably 10 years.

For the most part, everything works on Windows the same was as it does on Mac or Linux. On the few occasions where something is off, I've noted it, but generally what WSL2 buys you is compatibility with the rest of the computing landscape.

[a]https://docs.docker.com/engine/install/linux-postinstall/

You also don't need to be the most experienced developer. Some experience writing code in any language will be sufficient. The Docker stuff isn't really code. If you've never done Bash before, don't worry, that will all be explained, including some esoteric command line stuff that is notoriously hard to search for.

Typographical Conventions

As a book that must work on lots of devices *and* paper, the code listings have to fit in a certain space. I've done my best to make sure the code is accurate and doesn't flow off the page.

There are some command-line invocations, and they look like so:

```
> ls -xF /
bin@   boot/  dev/  etc/  home/  lib@  media/  mnt/  opt/  p. . .
sbin@  srv/   sys/  tmp/  usr/   var/
```

Sometimes, the output is lengthy and irrelevant, so in those cases, it's omitted, and would look like so:

```
> ls /etc
«lots of output»
```

More frequently, a command-line invocation will be long, and not fit on the page. Fortunately, the UNIX command-line environment allows you to stretch a command over several lines by ending a line in a backslash. For example:

```
> ls -l ~/projects
```

Can be written as:

```
> ls \
  -l \
  ~/projects
```

For code, when creating a file, the text should state clearly to create a file with a given name in a given location. For example, I might ask you to create the file `amazing.js` in the current directory:

```
/* amazing.js */

document.addEventListener("DOMContentLoaded", () => {
  console.log("This is the only JS in this book")
})
```

For editing code, I'll try to show enough context to know where to make edits, along with arrows that indicate the changed code:

```
/* amazing.js */

  document.addEventListener("DOMContentLoaded", () => {
→   console.log("I lied, this is also JS")
→   console.log("And sorry in advance, there is gonna be YAML")
  })
```

Sometimes lines of output are too long for the page but also not relevant. Those will be truncated and I assure you that there is no important information being lost.

One last thing that I cannot seem to fix is that copy and paste out of the PDF is often somewhat strange. I would recommend you type things out. It's better for learning anyway. If you don't want to type things out, the sample code is available from the book's website at `https://devbox.computer/sample_code.zip`.

If you have any problems getting things to work, try the sample code from the website first.

OK, let's get into it. What exactly *is* a dev environment?

2 A Dev Environment Defined

I don't want to code anything, download anything, or compile anything as a programmer. I don't want to code anything downloaded or compiled, or download anything coded or compiled, or compile anything downloaded, transpiled, or coded, or fix anything coded, compiled, or downloaded. You know, as a programmer, I don't want to do that.

—excerpt from "The Career Programmer", by Lloyd Dobler

A dev environment is everything you need to write and maintain an app, along with a workflow for doing development. Some parts of a dev environment are specific to your app, but a fair bit actually aren't.

2.1 Where Work is Done - The Foundational Layers of a Dev Environment

Before any commands or code editing can be done, the work of software development needs a place to happen. This place has two parts: a *Foundational Core* that contains the operating system, programming language runtimes, and services your app needs (like databases), and a *Workspace* which is the source code, test data, and other artifacts specific to your app.

The dev environment is shown in "Foundations of a Dev Environment" on the next page.

The *Foundational Core* is what this book is about, and includes

- the operating system.
- programming language runtimes and standard libraries.
- general tools needed for development, like headless browsers, databases, or caches.

While the specific elements of the foundational core might be particular to your app—for example, it requires Ruby 3.2 or Postgres 13—the tools themselves are generic across similar apps. Ruby 3.2 is the same for every app that uses Ruby 3.2. Thus, what you'll learn in this book will be the skills to set up any foundational core for any app's needs.

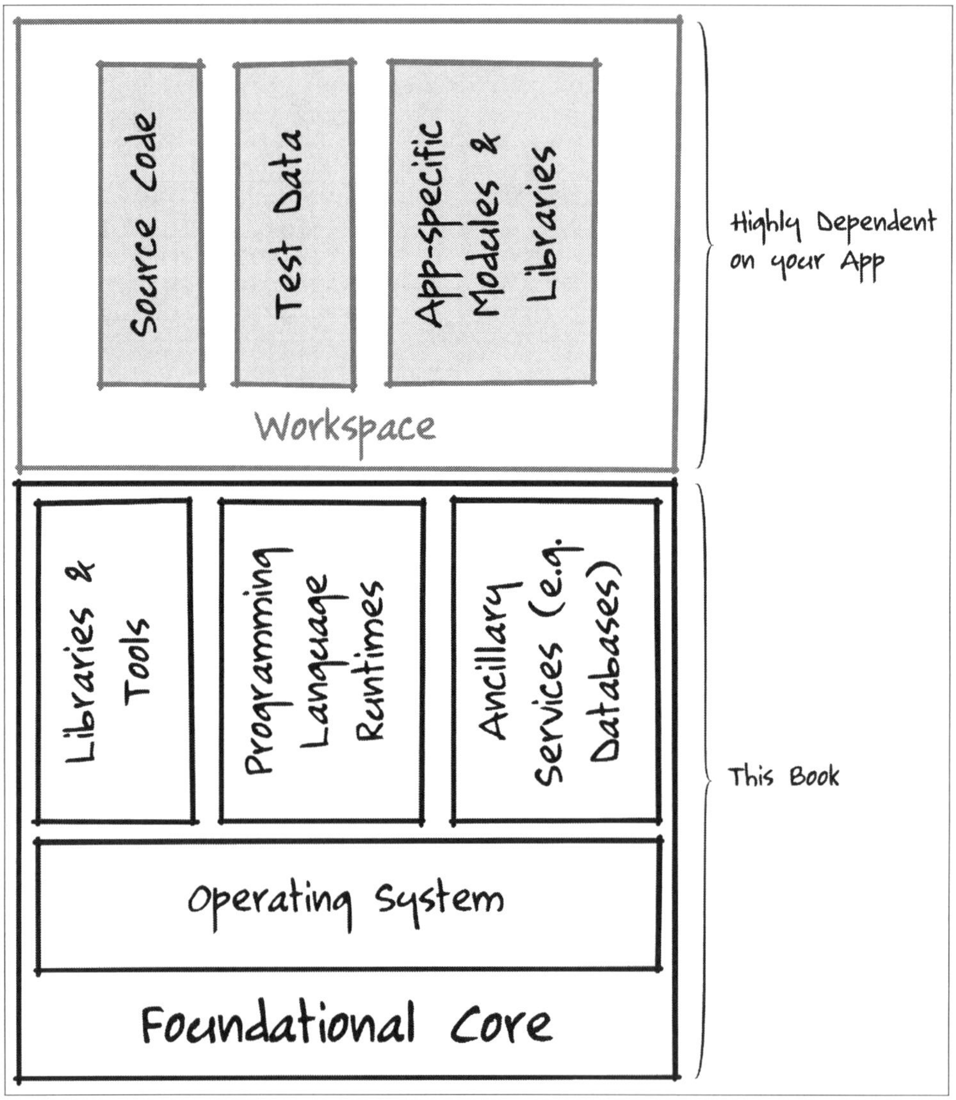

Figure 2.1: Foundations of a Dev Environment

The *Workspace*, however, is highly specific to your app, and includes

- the app's source code.
- test data or other artifacts the app needs to run.
- modules or libraries upon which the app is built, usually managed by a package manager.

While we can't make a generic tools to manage a Workspace like we can the Foundational Core, we *will* learn some Bash and this can be applied to your app's Workspace. The appendix "A Protocol for Dev Environments" on page 129 will outline a standard set of scripts you can define to create a Workspace consistent with other Workspaces.

I will acknowledge that the line between the Foundational Core and the Workspace can be blurry. Most developers prefer to have as many dependencies as possible be managed by the app's source code and, thus, in the Workspace. Not everything can be managed this way. For example, I needed to use ImageMagick on a Ruby project. While there is a Ruby library that *wraps* ImageMagick, that library cannot install ImageMagick. That had to be installed at the OS level—the Foundational Core.

Even though you will want your Foundational Core to be as minimal as you can make it, you never know what you're going to need to install there, and we'll learn a general process for making that happen. As the title of this book suggests, we'll be creating the Foundational Core with Docker, and we'll use Bash to provide a great user interface for it. Yes, Bash.

Aside form the Foundational Core and Workspace, we also want to think about our dev workflow.

2.2 How Work is Done - The Workflows of a Dev Environment

No matter what sort of app you are working on, you will usually follow these steps:

1. Install your operating system.
2. Set up the Foundational Core by installing necessary language runtimes, common tools, and services (like databases).
3. Pull down the app's source code and run any app-specific setup like installing libraries or setting up test data.
4. Work on the app by making changes to it, running its tests, and pushing changes back to a shared repo or do whatever needs doing on the app itself.

Typically, Steps 1 and 2 happen infrequently, which is part of the reason they are always not quite correct. Steps 3 and 4 are activities you'll perform much more frequently. What we'll learn is how to fully automate and script steps 1 and 2. These skills can be applied to making steps 3 and 4 more streamlined as well.

As a preview, this is how it will look:

`dx/build` Install an OS and Foundational Core into a disk image.

`dx/start` Use that disk image to start a virtual computer.

`git fetch` Update your app's source code on your computer's disk.

`dx/exec «some command»` Run any comand inside the virtual computer, such as tests.

These will be polished scripts that don't require arguments and perform all the necessary steps without requiring you to consult any documentation.

These steps hint at our solution (which is more than hinted at by the title of this book): we're doing to use virtualization and automation to manage our dev environment. To see the reasoning and benefits, let's look at the four ways in which dev environments are often managed.

3

The Four Types of Dev Environments

Pai Mei brought Kiddo to the standing desk. On the desk was a brand new computer. Kiddo tried to install the latest version of NodeJS following Pai Mei's written instructions. When it failed, she turned to her master. Pai Mei only frowned.
Kiddo, unsure how to proceed, said "Master, how am I to install software onto my computer?"
*Pai Mei, enraged, smashed her knuckles with the end of his staff. "*Your *computer?"*
Cradling her bruised hand, Kiddo cried: "Master, is it not mine?!"
Pai Mei, still enraged, again smashed Kiddo's hand with his staff. After a single stroke of his long, white beard, he simply grumbled and glared at Kiddo.
Kiddo's eyes dropped as she looked back at the computer. Her gnarled fingers could barely enter the search terms into the operating system vendor's support site. In that moment, she was enlightened.

—*Kill Bill, Vol 3*

While there are actually an *infinite* number of dev environments, any given setup can be categorized along two axes, to give us four broad categories. This chapter explains why one of these is superior to the others.

First, a dev environment is categorized based on the instructions for setting it up: documentation on one side and automation on the other. I'd bet most environments you've used were heavy on documentation and light on automation.

The second axis relates to how the environment is run. Is it native—running everything directly on the developer's workstation—or virtual—running in the cloud or a virtual environment?

What we're building in this book is the best of the four options: automated and virtualized. Let's talk through why automation is better than documentation and virtualization is better than native.

3.1 The Best Documentation is an Executable Script

Documentation is cheap to produce, especially if it isn't maintained or well-written. It's often better than nothing, so most teams start their journey to a sustainable dev environment with a Markdown file or a wiki that outlines what you need to do to get set up. This does not scale. At all.

It's extremely hard to write good documentation. It's harder when what you are documenting is complex, which happens when your software installation system has to accommodate several package managers, operating systems, hardware architectures, and Pat, who insists on building everything from source.

Of course, even if you could achieve this, how is this documentation maintained? For dev environments, the new hires are usually charged with updating it when they find it doesn't work. Over time, the steps become so convoluted that not even the most conscientious person can follow them.

Automation solves this. Automation shows exactly what has to happen because it makes it happen. Automation either works or doesn't. Even though automation feels expensive to produce, it saves time the more it's used.

Automation has two further advantages. First, developers already possess the skills to produce it, whereas they may or may not be good at writing. Second, automation can be tested. A script that sets up a working dev environment can be used to setup an environment for continuous integration, thus ensuring that the team is aware of issues quickly, and can fix them just as quickly.

3.2 Our Computers are Increasingly Not Under Our Control

If you happen to be a Ruby developer who uses a Mac, you've no-doubt experienced the yearly problem when macOS releases an update and you can no longer install Ruby. Macs have long-since stopped shipping with a reasonable version of Ruby, and you certainly can't install gems (Ruby's form of third-party libraries) without breaking something.

This is not something unique to Apple. Every OS vendor, in their quest for stability, will take great strides to prevent changes to what is considered the "system software". If some script depends on a particular version of Perl, and you change that version, you could break the operating system.

Of course, it's not just the operating system vendor. Many companies have IT and security teams tasked with preventing security incidents. A critical tool in doing so is to force operating system and software updates to the employees. These teams aren't always capable or incentivized to work with developers to ensure such updates won't impact their ability to work. Even if they did, at the end of the day, security updates are going to be more important.

The reality is that we don't really own all the software on our computers, and that we can't easily understand how the various libraries and tools that come with it are affected by the libraries and tools we need to do our work.

Virtualization solves this. As long as your computer can run the virtualization software, you can run a virtual machine configured exactly how you like, and it won't change out from under you. *And* your entire team can use that exact same version, even though said team might be using a myriad of different computers and operating systems.

Virtualization *does* come with potentially worse performance than running natively, but this is a worthwhile trade-off (and the performance gap is always shrinking). I would be willing to bet that the time spent waiting for slightly slower tests is far outweighed by the time saved not wrestling with some arcane compiler flags every time something changes in your OS.

3.3 Automation and Virtualization Lead to Sustainability

An automated dev environment, based on virtualized operating systems, provides a solid foundation for building just about any app. The automation is never out of date, and the operating system can be kept stable.

Eschewing virtualization requires automating the set up of a developer laptop. While this is better than a documentation-based approach, it's still highly complex. The automation must account for all operating systems and hardware.

When automating developer workstation setup, the team must either maintain that system themselves or rely on a third party. Whatever preconceived notions you may have about Docker, I can assure you that it's simpler to have Docker install software than to write a script that must work across many different OSes and hardware profiles.

As for third party solutions, they have to get installed themselves *and* the team must understand how they work to debug or enhance them. This turns out to be more difficult than learning a commonly-used tool like Docker. We'll talk about this in "Tech Companies Should Not Own Your Dev Environment" on page 119.

On the other side, using a virtualized environment with documented instructions can be helpful, but you still fall victim to the trappings of documentation. Your docs might be simpler, since they can address the virtualized environment only, but they will still fall out of date.

We're going to use Docker for virtualization, and a combination of Docker and Bash for automation. The reasons have to do with a hidden, third axis: how easy is it to understand the abstractions on which your dev environment is built?

3.4 You Must Always Understand One Level Below the Current Abstraction

The best abstractions are borne from repeated applications of a technology for a well-defined use-case. Writing assembly language gets tiresome, so C was invented. Even though assembly can do far more than C, for most common use-cases, C is much faster and easier to use. It's a great abstraction.

If you learn C and not assembly, you will eventually hit a limit. You won't know exactly what problem C was created to solve and, eventually, there will be a problem that your knowledge of C alone cannot solve. You will need to learn a bit of assembly.

Your dev environment is the same way. Whatever mechanism you use to manage it, it is ultimately an abstraction on top of other technologies that are being orchestrated to manage your environment. When something goes wrong—either due to a bug or an unforeseen use case—you'll need to pop the hood and see what's under there.

Thus, you need to understand—or be able to get an understanding of—whatever your dev environment is built on, as shown in "Understanding Abstractions" below.

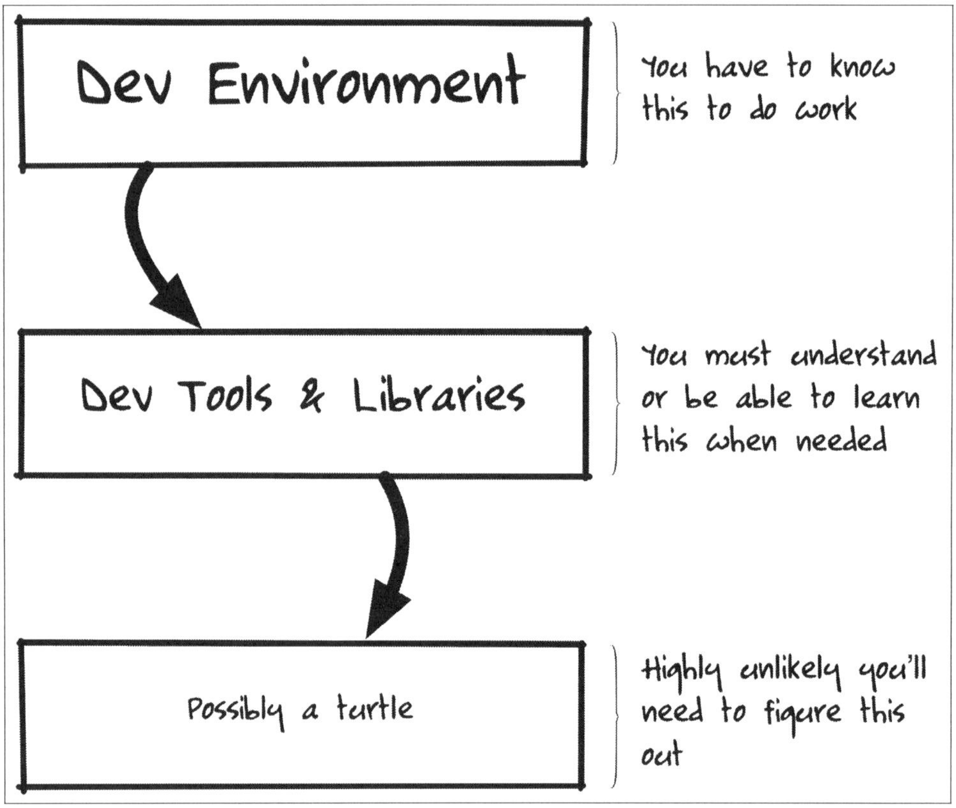

Figure 3.1: Understanding Abstractions

What *this* means is that your dev environment should use technologies that you either do, or can, understand. Applying this to your team, this also implies that there is more value in using commonly-understood, battle-tested technologies than in using something that might tick off more features but is more esoteric or less likely to continue to exist past its next round of funding.

Docker—despite being VC-funded itself—is prolific. A *lot* of people understand it, and it's not going anywhere. There are even competing products that can build Docker images and run Docker containers.

And Bash... well... Bash will outlive us all. The only better investment in your career than learning Bash is learning SQL and if there were a way to automate all this with SQL, I'd *definitely* be considering it.

To that end, we'll now start our journey to learn this stuff. It's not going to take too long. We'll start with Docker, which, despite some warts and a few design flaws, is the best tool for the job of virtualizing our dev environment.

4

What is Docker and How Does It Work?

> *Most computer programming is based on copy and paste. It's so easy to civilize by teaching copy and paste. You water down the standards which would lead to reading the docs. You restrain the will. You regulate the appetites. You fence in the horizons. You make a Stack Overflow answer for every problem. You deny the existence of the source code. You teach even the children to use ChatGPT. You tame.*
>
> —*God Emperor of Dune, Early Draft*

So what is Docker? Like all good venture-backed companies, their home page has lots of animations, big fonts, a splashy design, but not a lot of complete sentences. Here's the first one I could find, halfway down the page:

> Docker provides a suite of development tools, services, trusted content, and automations, used individually or together, to accelerate the delivery of secure applications.

This is technically true, but not particularly enlightening. At its core, Docker is a piece of software that runs other software as if it were executing inside a virtual machine. But Docker is also an ecosystem of virtual machine images that we can use. And use them we will.

Go ahead and install Docker[1]. You want to install "Docker Desktop", which provides the Docker Engine and a UI to help manage Docker on your computer.

While you are doing that, I want to go over some concepts and terminology. Like all good computer systems, Docker has chosen words for its concepts that are often in contravention of their intuitive meaning in other contexts.

Docker exists to run virtual computers[2] called *containers*. They may be created, stopped, started, or destroyed, just like a real computer. They are based on an *image*.

---

[1] https://docs.docker.com/get-docker/

[2] I assure you, I understand the difference between a Docker container and a virtual computer. This difference is not as meaningful as it may seem, and is a key contributor to most people's difficulty in understanding Docker.

4.1 Images are Cloned Hard Drives

A Docker image is a set of bytes that can be used to create one or more containers. Think of it like the image of a hard drive that you then clone to create multiple computers. You'd use an image to *create* a container, which can then be *started* or later *stopped.*

An image is *built* based a Dockerfile. A *Dockerfile* is a glorified shell script that controls what goes into the image. It usually specifies a base image and then some commands for installing software into that base.

For example, you may start with a Debian Linux base image, and then install NodeJS onto that. The resulting image, when started as a container, would have NodeJS installed on it.

You can also fetch images from the Internet. This is one of the most powerful aspects of using Docker (and also its most confusing and error-prone). Docker Hub hosts myriad images for every conceivable piece of software. Many of them are maintained by the vendor, so if you want the canonical way to run MySQL[3], you can fetch a MySQL image from Docker Hub that the MySQL team published there. This repository of images is called, naturally, a *container registry.*

Wait, what?

4.2 Nothing is Registered with the Container Registry, but if Something Were Registered, it Would Definitely Not Be Containers. This is Fine.

Yup, a container registry really is where images are stored. To make matters worse, you don't actually *register* images, either. You *push* them. I guess this is supposed to be analogous to Git?

A pushed image can be immediately fetched, which is called *pulling.* This is another Git analogy, and a broken one. Pulling a Docker image is more like *fetching* in Git, insomuch as it retrieves some info and puts it somewhere out of your way. Pulling in Git makes a mess[4].

Sometimes, you will see the phrase "pull from the registry", but sometimes you'll see "pull from the repository" (or "repo"). A *repository* stores different versions of the same image, though the images are not versioned in the way.

For example, there are images that can run both Redis 6 and Redis 7 stored in the "redis" repository of the Docker Hub container registry. These images aren't versioned, and we'll talk about how you can try to identify which is which in "You Want Versions, But Docker Provides Only Tags" on page 24 . For now, a repo is where a bunch of images that purport to be the same thing are grouped. In the container registry.

---

[3]You don't. Please use Postgres.

[4]If you regularly run `git pull`, I admire your risk-loving lifestyle and sense of adventure. The first time I trashed by local copy by doing a `git pull` I vowed never to run it again, and I haven't. It's been 16 years. 16 safe years.

4.3 The Host is Your Computer

Almost everywhere in computer software, a *host* runs some sort of service you connect to. In Docker, *host* means "whatever is running the Docker Engine". In the context of a dev environment, "host" is *your computer*. This still confuses me, and I can't believe they couldn't come up with a better term. I would've gone with "Docker Engine", but that is a lot more letters to type out, and programmers hate typing out things[5].

Your computer—the host—will need to access services running inside containers. This requires understanding ports.

4.4 Ports are not Mapped, But Published (or Exposed)

Docker provides a way to map a host port (i.e. a port on your computer's `localhost`) to a port in the container. This is called *publishing*. And before you ask, no, I don't know why they didn't go with "mapping".

But that's not all you can do with ports! We'll also set up a virtual network of Docker containers in "Running Databases and Caches with One Line of Code" on page 49. A container can *expose* a port which makes it visible to the other containers, but not to your computer. This is a safer way to map ports, and we'll discuss it later[6].

4.5 Disks are Called Volumes... Sometimes. But They Definitely Are Never Called Disks

The last term for now is *volume* which is the Docker word for "disk". While I'd agree that "disk image" could be conflated with "image", "volume" should've been called "disk"[7]. Nevertheless, volumes are how you save bytes to a disk so those bytes can exist outside any containers you may have started or stopped.

Containers *do* have internal storage, but any bytes written to that storage are effectively ephemeral. They can persist if a specific container continues to exist, but containers themselves are somewhat ephemeral, so you generally don't want to rely on putting bytes into a container. Any bytes you care about it being there must be in the *image*.

Sometimes, you do need bytes to sit around on disk for long periods of time. Volumes make that possible.

We'll mostly be using volumes to allow a running container to access our app's source code that lives on the host (your computer). This is called *mounting* a volume (which comes from the UNIX term for mounting a disk). Volumes can be used in a ton of other ways, and this makes anything to do with volumes complicated. But we'll get through it.

[5] They didn't try hard enough to make "D10e" happen.

[6] To really underscore how bad these names are, if you had to choose which is more dangerous or risky, I'd go with "exposing". You don't want to be "exposed", generally speaking. And yet, *exposing* ports in Docker is generally safer and less risky than publishing.

[7] I guess I should be glad it's not called "block storage" because, wow, what a terrible name.

The figure "Docker Concepts" below, ties this all together, and the terms are summarized in "The Docker Lexicon for Regular People" on page 123

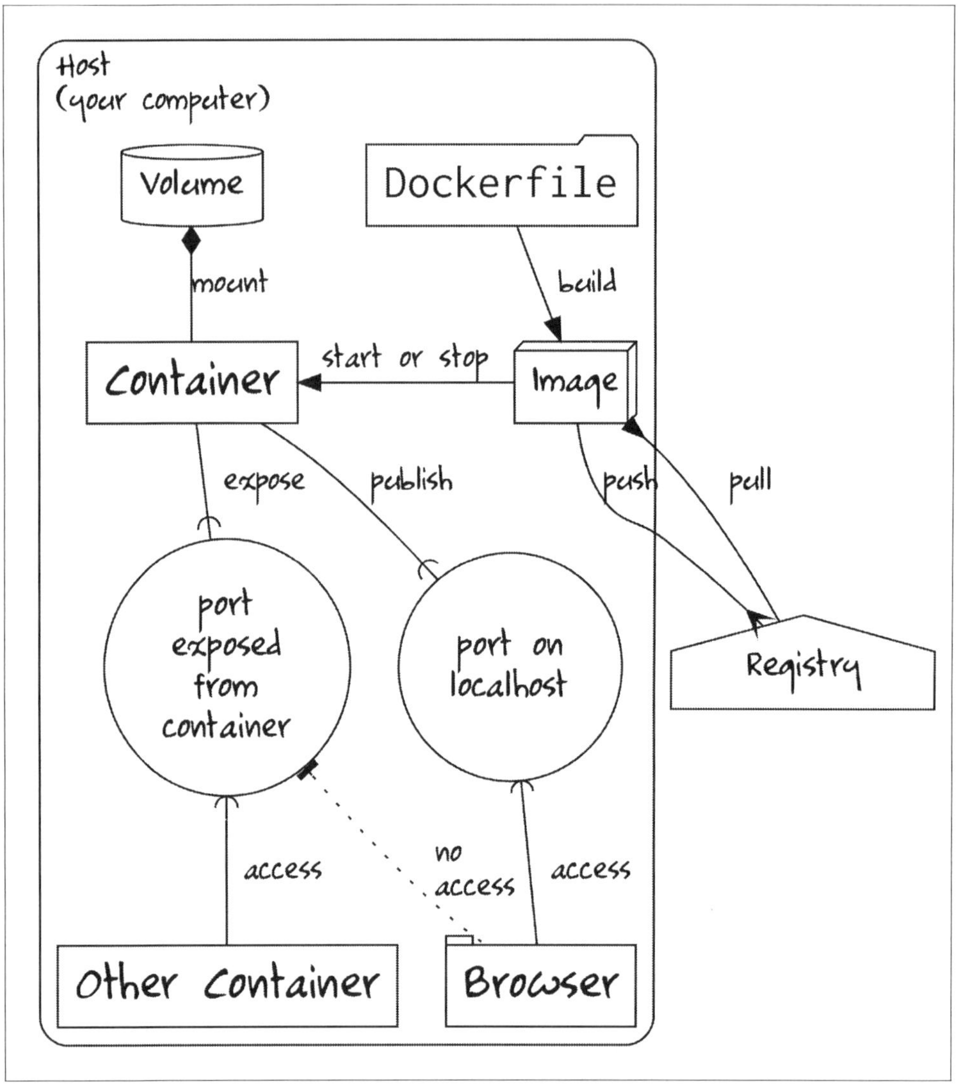

Figure 4.1: Docker Concepts

Keep this chapter handy while we soldier on. In the next chapter we'll actually build an image, start a container, and see things happening. We'll start by talking about how to manage the lowest level of the Foundational Core: the operating system.

5

Managing the Operating System With Base Images

Obi-wan flipped on Luke's content blockers. Luke asked "with these blockers on, how am I supposed to read the documentation?" Without missing a beat, Obi-wan responded: "Websites can deceive you... don't trust them. Stretch out with your feelings!" Luke found a Docker image that felt right. He downloaded it. Obi-wan, seeing this, reassured him: "See, you can do it!"

—Dialogue from Obi-Wan Season 2 sizzle reel

Since you've got Docker installed, let's see it in action. This will be a jumping-off point for learning more, so let's try it now:

```
> docker run debian uname -a
Linux dd8c32c549cf 6.4.16-linuxkit #1 SMP PREEMPT Thu Nov 16. . .
```

The first time you do this, it will take a while. Like... a while. It's downloading an image named "debian" from the default container registry, Docker Hub[1]. That image contains an entire operating system in it. Once it's downloaded, Docker will use that image to create a container that it will then start and run `uname -a` in. The container will then stop. You should see a similar output to what's above. Neat!

But hold up, what's all this about "run"? We didn't talk about *running* things! This is for a good reason. The term *run* means: "pull the image if needed, then create a container based on it, then start that container, then execute that command inside the container, then stop the container". We are not ever going to use `docker run` again, nor are we going to use this term.

I had you use `docker run` for a reason. It is a warning. Docker's terms and documentation contain land mines. While some phrases like "creating a container" have a precise meaning, others do not.

"Run" is such a term. Docker themselves can't even define it. If you execute `docker run --help`, you will be be told that this command will "Create and *run* a new

[1]https://hub.docker.com/search

container from an image" (emphasis mine). `docker run` actually creates and *starts* a container from an image. Details matter.

Despite this, it *is* pretty cool that you can start a virtual machine from a single command. This shows you that, despite some aesthetic warts, Docker is gonna be really nice for making our dev environment.

The first part of that is the operating system upon which we'll base everything else. This is, refreshingly, called a *base image*, and we're going to go deep on how to choose that. Doing this involves a few steps: choosing an operating system, establishing a chain of trust from the OS vendor to a Docker Image, and then figuring out which specific image to use.

5.1 Choosing an Operating System

The first line of almost every Dockerfile specifies the base image using `FROM`. `FROM` is a *directive* that tells Docker what to do when building an image:

```
FROM «image name»
```

For example:

```
FROM debian
```

How do we figure out the image name? Even though we are not building something for a production workload, we *definitely* do not want to get our image name from some blog post, Stack Overflow, or GitHub Copilot. As you'll learn, the image name can be a vector for all sorts of unintended and hard-to-observe behavior. Thus, we must choose... wisely.

Before figuring out the image name we need to know what operating system we're going to use. There are three pieces of information relevant to this decision:

- Do you have technical requirements related to the OS?
- What OS are you running in production?
- What software do you need for development, and what OSes are supported?

In this book, we're going to choose Debian Linux. Debian is extremely popular, well maintained, and most software packages document how to install their software on Debian. This means we'll have the simplest time with each step of our dev environment's setup.

If you aren't sure what to choose, choose Debian. But, if you *do* have some technical need to use another OS, or you want to try to have some sort of parity with production, use that distribution instead.

One thing to be aware of that we will discuss in "Processor Architecture Issues" on page 116 is processor architecture. While your Apple Silicon Mac may technically be able to run an Intel-based virtual computer, you do not want to do this. It's slow and buggy.

It's likely you are running your production app on an Intel-based processor, so it may seem like a good idea to run that for development, too. It's a better trade-off to instead run production's OS built for your computer's processor, even if that's not the same as production's. You won't have to worry about this for the most part, as Docker's default behavior is to download an image built for your processor.

To figure out the actual images to use, we need to establish a chain of trust from Debian to Docker Hub.

5.2 Finding Images You Can Trust

When you run a command like `docker run debian «some command»`, Docker will find an image on Docker Hub and download it. If you were to mistype that and execute `docker run dabuan`, and there was an image with that name on Docker Hub, Docker would download it. This is relevant because anyone can push an image up to Docker Hub with any name that's not already taken[2].

This means you want to be sure you understand what you are downloading and running. Even though this is just dev, you don't want a typo to cause a state-based actor to have all of your source code.

Unfortunately, Docker doesn't provide much in the way of establishing a chain of trust between OS vendors and Docker images.

For building a dev environment, you have to make two assumptions:

- Any given vendor's website is not compromised, and the information on it is trustworthy.
- Docker Hub is not compromised.

These two assumptions mean if a vendor's website points you to a `hub.docker.com` URL, you can trust that the vendor is OK with using whatever you find at that URL. This logic isn't foolproof, but it's enough for our purposes[3]. If you instead use an image based on a Google search, you don't have any idea what might be in it, as shown in "Chain of Trust" on the next page.

Searching Debian's website for this information isn't easy. Their download page doesn't mention Docker, and their search engine doesn't return any useful results. Using Google, however, brings me to `wiki.debian.org/Docker`[4], which then links to `hub.docker.com/_/debian`[5]. The text on Debian's wiki is a strong indicator that they trust and approve of these images.

---

[2]You may want to look up "software supply chain attack".

[3]These assumptions are maybe not enough for production. I honestly do not know how any public or otherwise regulated company would ever, in a million years, not build their images from scratch.

[4]https://wiki.debian.org/Docker

[5]https://hub.docker.com/_/debian/

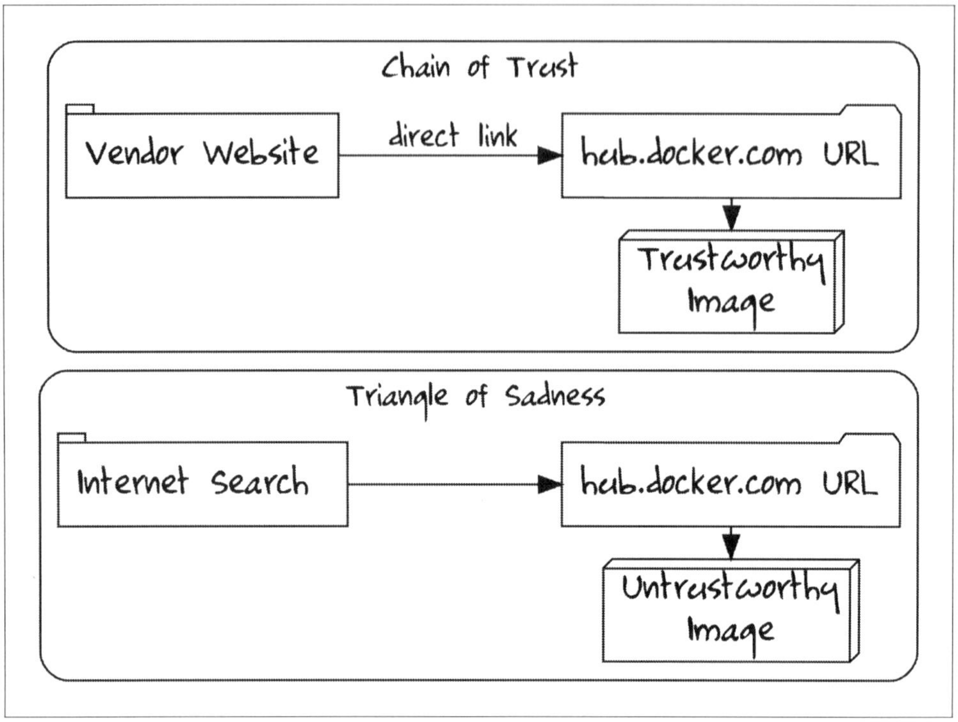

Figure 5.1: Chain of Trust

Even though the route was circuitous, this journey establishes a reasonable chain of trust from the vendor's website to Docker's. It's clear that the images at `hub.docker.com/_/debian` are intended, by Debian, to be the correct images to run Debian Linux via Docker.

Now, we need to learn how to decode what's on the Docker web page we just found.

5.3 You Want Versions, But Docker Provides Only Tags

Ideally, we want to specify a version of Debian Linux to use. Following the logic above for how to choose an OS, choosing the version is a similar set of steps. Are their technical requirements? What are we using in production? Otherwise, choose the *latest stable version*.

I emphasized "latest stable version" for a reason. Not every release of every operating system (or piece of software) is considered stable for use. For example, Ubuntu Linux has odd-numbered releases that are considered *previews* of upcoming stable releases. When the stable release happens, the version number is an even number. The odd-numbered images are then removed from Docker Hub. Ask me how I know.

After understanding the Vendor's versioning scheme, it's not exactly clear how to choose an image name, even though the images sorta, kinda, if you squint hard enough, contain version numbers. The problem is, they don't. They are tags, which are not immutable.

The page we got to on `hub.docker.com` is generated by Docker based on what is provided by Debian. If you scroll past the tags, you will see some documentation, and in there it tells you a bit about how it all works. It's not very clear, but what Debian does is a common way of mapping versions to tags, and you will find this mechanism in use broadly, even though it is not a feature of Docker (or an invention of Debian).

The tags represent the latest release within a scope. For example, the tag `12` will always be the most recently-released version Debian Linux, version 12. However, `12.1` would only be the most recently-released version that starts with 12.1. See Debian Tagging Strategy below for how the tags change over time.

The figure shows that in July, the tags `bookworm`, `12`, and `12.1` all point to the image that is version `12.1.0` of Debian Linux.

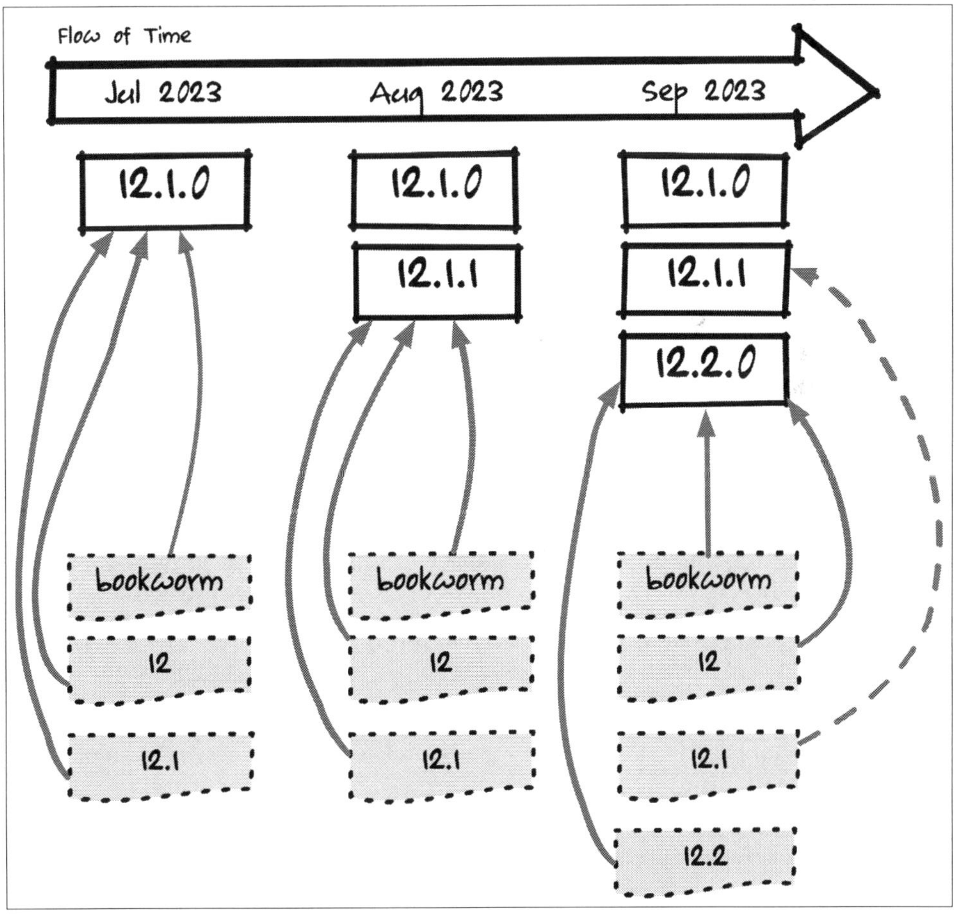

Figure 5.2: Debian Tagging Strategy

In August, 12.1.1 is released. Debian will change where the tags point so that all three—`bookworm`, `12`, and `12.1`—now point to 12.1.1. In September, when 12.2 is released, `bookworm` and `12` will change to point to 12.2.0, but `12.1` will *remain* pointing at the most recent version of 12.1, which is 12.1.1. A new tag is created—`12.2`—to point to 12.2.0. This tag will move with any 12.2.x version.

I want to emphasize that this behavior is *entirely up to the vendor*. This is not a supported feature of Docker. It's basically a hack to be able to communicate versions to users given the fact that Docker doesn't support versions for images.

This means that if you download the image tagged with 12 today, someone downloading the image tagged with 12 tomorrow could get something different. This happened to me when writing this book; Debian removed `curl` from their base image even though I didn't change the image name I was using.

Let's choose the latest version of Debian, which is 12, but constrain it to the first point release, just to have *some* constraints on what is changed when team members build their images. Thus, we'll use the tag `12.1`. This makes our image name `debian:12.1`.

So, what happened at the start of this chapter, when we used the image name `debian`? I'll tell you: we inadvertently triggered a pretty serious design flaw in Docker: the `latest` tag.

5.4 Never, Ever, Ever—and I do Mean *Ever*—Use the `latest` Tag

You can use the command `docker image ls` to see all the images that have been downloaded to your computer. You can give this command an image name and it will show information about only that image. Let's do that now:

```
> docker image ls debian
REPOSITORY   TAG      IMAGE ID       CREATED        SIZE
debian       latest   60e0ade36b1a   4 months ago   139MB
```

You'll notice a few things. First, the name "debian" is under the heading "REPOSITORY". Under the heading "TAG" is the word "latest". These two values are combined with a colon to form the name of the image, in this case `debian:latest`.

As it turns out, all Docker image names *must* contain exactly one colon where the part before the colon is the "repository" and the part *after* the colon is the "tag".

Here is Docker's design flaw: if you are specifying an image name, and do not use a colon, Docker will silently add `:latest` to the image name. This means that `docker run debian uname -a` is the same as `docker run debian:latest uname -a`. The reason this is such a serious mistake on Docker's part is that the `latest` tag *in no way represents the latest of anything*. It's a tag like any other.

For example, if you work for Debian Linux, you could grab a very old unsupported version, create a Docker image, and push it up without using a colon, and *that version* is tagged `latest`. Or, you could grab a random version from your computer, and push that with the tag `latest` explicitly, and then *that* would be `latest`. Latest what?

You are possibly familiar with Isaac Asimov's "Three Laws of Robotics"[6]. I will present to you his lesser known, easier to follow, Single Law of Docker:

> Do not use the `latest` tag, or, through inaction, allow the `latest` tag to be used.

The `latest` tag is absolute poison and Docker should deprecate it.

Next, we'll make our Dockerfile by specifying the base image we've chosen and installing the necessary software.

[6]https://en.wikipedia.org/wiki/Three_Laws_of_Robotics

6

Installing Software in the Dev Environment

The temporal surge we detected was caused by an explosion of a single line of Bash passing through `curl`*. Somehow, the code emitted by the script shifted the disk sectors in our secondary storage into a high state of temporal polarization.*

—Miles O'Brien, Deep Space Nine, Season 5 Rejected Episode, "The Prophet and the Docker Hub"

In the last chapter, I mentioned that `FROM` is called a "directive". A Dockerfile will have other directives, the most notable of which is `RUN`. `RUN` accepts a command-line invocation and runs that against the current version of the image being built. As we'll see, some of these invocations are quite complex and this is why a Dockerfile really is a glorified shell script.

By the end of this chapter, we'll have a working Dockerfile we can use to run an app I created for this book. The app uses Ruby, a library called Sinatra, an unreleased CSS framework I built called Melange, and requires `esbuild` as part of the dev environment to manage front-end assets. Sounds great, doesn't it?

The reason for this mishmash of tools is to demonstrate the power of using Docker to manage a dev environment. Our Dockerfile will allow anyone to get going with this app, even if they don't have any clue how Ruby works or why you need to have a build tool for a CSS library.

In building the Dockerfile, we'll learn about *layers*, which is a mechanism Docker uses to optimize image build speed and disk space. We'll also learn how to follow a similar chain of trust regarding installation of software, much like we did when choosing a base image.

6.1 The App We'll Build to Make My Cats Say Things

Before any of that, find a place on your computer to work, and get the source code for the example app. You can download it from the book's website `https://devbox.computer/sample_code.zip` or install Git[1], and clone the app's code from GitHub[2].

[1] https://github.com/git-guides/install-git
[2] https://github.com/davetron5000/catsay

```
> git clone https://github.com/davetron5000/catsay.git
Cloning into 'catsay'...
```

The app, called CatSay, is a basic web app that allows you to provide two pieces of text that will then be rendered as if my two cats—Carlos Rosario and Zoni—are saying them[3].

You will notice that CatSay has a pretty basic README that outlines the software dependencies it has: Ruby and NodeJS. It also talks about "RubyGems" and "Node modules". These are part of the app's Workspace (as discussed in chapter 2 on page 7) and are managed by the files `Gemfile` and `package.json`, respectively.

The README indicates that `bin/setup` will install RubyGems and Node Modules, so our job is to get a Docker image created so that can happen. This means we'll need Ruby and NodeJS installed.

6.2 Establish a Chain of Trust for Software Installation

Just as we established a link from Debian's website to Docker Hub (see the previous chapter on page 23), we now need to find a link from the software vendor's site to installation instructions (in our case, for Debian Linux).

This link should be direct, so we can trust that the way we are going to install the software on our chosen operating system is reliable. If you get instructions from a blog post or large-language model, you really don't have any idea what you've installed, as shown in "Software Chain of Trust" on the next page.

Let's start with Ruby, which has a home on the Internet at `www.ruby-lang.org`. If you click "Download Ruby", then "Installation", then "Debian, Ubuntu", you will end up at `www.ruby-lang.org/en/documentation/installation/#apt`.

This shows us that the installation instructions are `apt-get install ruby-full`. But, if you were reading the pages that you clicked on to get here, you may have noticed this text (emphasis mine):

> On a UNIX-like operating system, using your system's package manager is easiest. However, the packaged Ruby version *may not be the newest one.*

This may or may not matter, but we should at least figure out what version *would* be installed. You can start by going to `www.debian.org/distrib/packages`, scrolling down and entering "ruby-full" into the search form. That should bring you to `packages.debian.org/bookworm/ruby-full`. Note that "bookworm" is the name of version 12, which is explained on the Docker Hub page for the Debian images.

This page says that it provides Ruby 3.1, which is fine for our purposes. If we wanted the latest Ruby, we would need to explore other options from `ruby-lang.org` and follow them.

[3] If you are a venture capitalist, please don't bother reaching out. CatSay is a lifestyle business and I can't let myself succumb the pressures of delivering year-over-year margins of 30% or higher.

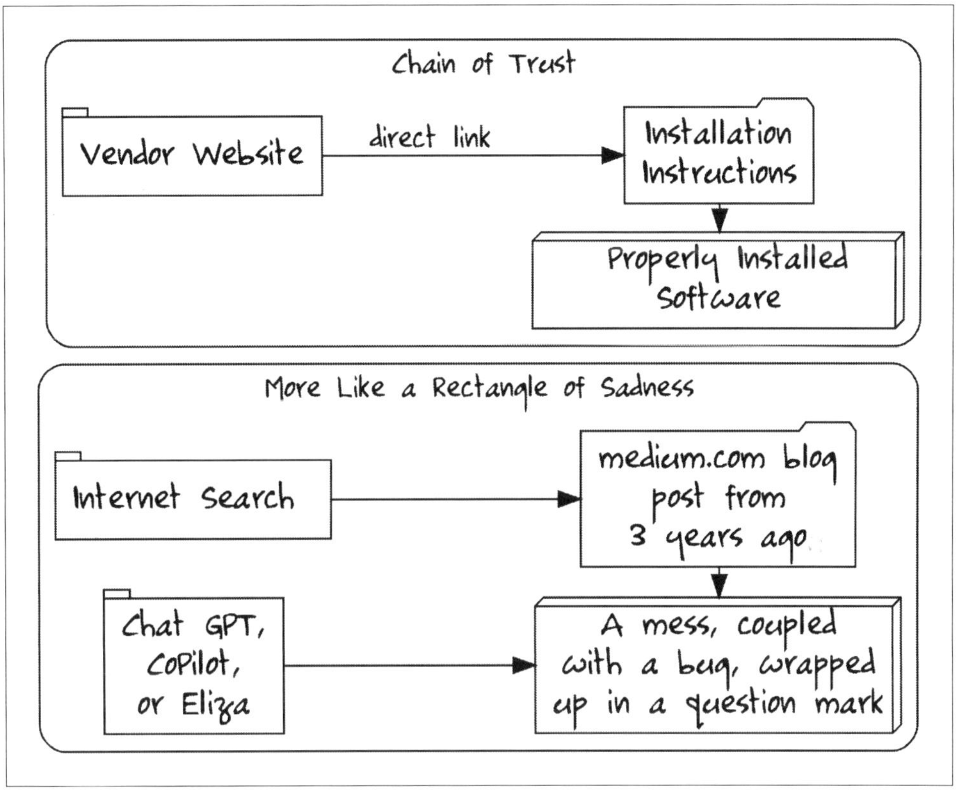

Figure 6.1: Software Chain of Trust

If you aren't using Debian, hopefully the installation instructions are similarly straightforward. In any case, you need to know how the package manager works for your chosen OS. For Debian, you are wise to run `apt-get update` at the top of each Dockerfile to ensure the freshly-installed OS has an updated list of all available packages.

Before we add this to the Dockerfile, I'm going to save you a bit of heartache related to Ruby. We need to also install the package `build-essential`. This package contains a bunch of stuff for compiling C programs. This is relevant because some popular Ruby libraries are actually wrappers for C code, and that requires compilation as part of the install process. And, because Debian doesn't include such tools by default, we need to install them.

Another thing Debian no longer includes by default is `curl` (as I mentioned when discussing Docker's non-versioned tagging system on page 24). `curl` fetches URLs from the internet and is commonly used to download software outside of Debian's packaging system. We'll need to do that later, so we also need to install `curl`.

Docker can't—and no tool really can—save you from some of this nonsense. By *automating* the nonsense, however, the entire team can be reap the benefits without having to update or follow documentation. And, since everyone is using the same operating system, the nonsense will only require one set of instructions.

With that, we are now ready to create our Dockerfile, which will be called `Dockerfile.dev` (to clearly indicate its purpose) and be placed at the root of where you checked out catsay. Let's see the code first and then dissect it:

```
# Dockerfile.dev

FROM debian:12.1

RUN apt-get update --quiet --yes

# curl is needed to install NodeJS
RUN apt-get install --quiet --yes curl

# From https://www.ruby-lang.org/en/documentation/installation/#apt
# NOTE: build-essential is needed to install Ruby C extensions
RUN apt-get install --quiet --yes ruby-full build-essential
```

The first line we discussed earlier, and this sets the base image to `debian:12.1`. Next, we have a `RUN` directive to update the local package list, as discussed. The second `RUN` installs curl. We have not established a chain of trust for `curl`, but since it was part of the default install and is still available via Debian's package manager, this should be fine.

The third `RUN` is where we install Ruby based on our trusted instructions. Note four things:

- We aren't using `sudo` because all commands run as `root` (UNIX superuser) by default, and `sudo` is only needed when running as non-`root`.
- We use `--quiet` to reduce output from the command and `--yes` to automatically answer "yes" to any interactive question the command will ask (if you omit this, building your image will hang and you will have no idea why).
- We precede the `RUN` directive with a link to where we got the instructions. *This is important* because it makes it easier to maintain the `Dockerfile.dev` in the future. It also acts as evidence that a chain of trust was established.
- The comment preceding `RUN` *also* includes an explanation for installing `build-essentials`. This is *also important* because you may or may not need those packages as the app evolves. Having an explanation of what they are for makes the file easier to manage.

If you have experience with `apt-get` or other command line tools, you may be thinking that instead of writing `apt-get update --quiet --yes`, you could write `apt-get update -qy`. You are right, but I would still recommend in Dockerfiles (and shell scripts) to use the long-form options. They are easier to search for when someone doesn't know what they mean, and they are intuitive enough to avoid having to even look up. It just takes a few extra keystrokes and can save so many headaches.

Even though we aren't quite ready to develop CatSay, let's go ahead and build this image and test it.

6.3 Building and Testing an Image

To build an image, you'll use `docker build`. `docker build` requires a few command line arguments to work. The most peculiar is `--tag` which is documented as "Name and optionally a tag (format: 'name:tag')". This is a minor design mistake on Docker's part. `--tag` specifies the image name, and the format of that name, as discussed in the previous chapter on page 26, is "repository:tag". And remember, the ":tag" part will be automatically specified as ":latest" if you omit it, but due to Asimov's First Law of Docker, you *must not let this happen.*

6.3.1 Naming Your Dev Image

You are almost always going to be using a single dev image per app, so you may consider naming your image something like `catsay:dev`. This has two problems. First, your production image might be named `catsay`, and that is a semantically different image than the one we are building. Second, you may want to run two versions of the dev image. Perhaps you are upgrading to the latest version of Debian and want to run both side by side? It's much easier to do that if the two images have different names.

My recommendation is to use `«app»-dev` for the repository part, and then a string containing critical versions of software in the tag part. For example, `catsay-dev:debian-12.2-ruby3.1`. For CatSay, let's assume that the OS is most critical, so we'll use `catsay-dev:debian-12.1`. Note that you can use a slash in the repository part, but some external services ascribe special meaning to this. For your development image, avoid slashes in the repository part of the name.

6.3.2 Building the Image

`docker build` also needs to be given a path to where a Dockerfile is and, if the Dockerfile is not named `Dockerfile`, the `--file` argument is required to tell it the name. Lastly, I'll be using `--quiet` to suppress the massive amount of output that I don't want included here, but you can omit that flag if you like.

Note that the command ends with a `.` (this can be easy to miss, but is required).

```
> docker build --quiet --file Dockerfile.dev --tag  \
  catsay-dev:debian-12.1 .
sha256:409b9632393c8d1c3caa6efe4601f486fc317bd711e300938fb84. . .
```

The output of `docker build` is a SHA256 hash of the image that was created. If you didn't use `--quiet`, you will see more output and the SHA is buried in a message that looks like this:

```
=> => writing image sha256:7ac13ccd08651f2cebd94c1061b4a1b. . .
```

The SHA uniquely identifies the image. If we make a change to `Dockerfile.dev` and rebuild, we'd get a new SHA256, even though the new image would have the same name as the original.

6.3.3 Using the Image to Create a Container

Now, let's create a container using this image. This is akin to cloning the internal drive of a new computer with one we have pre-built. `docker container create` is the command to use, and we'll give it the following information:

- The name of the image to use (this is required)
- A name for the container that will be created. This is optional, but is useful for interacting with the container later.
- A command that the container should run when it starts.

Unlike a normal computer, Docker containers don't sit idle - they need to be doing something. Of note, when the command we give the container completes, it will stop. We'll give our container `sleep infinity` to keep it running. This forces the container, when started, to sit idle, allowing us to issue it additional commands.

```
> docker container create --name catsay-container  \
  catsay-dev:debian-12.1 sleep infinity
6815f506509537a7a9adc222a5d7c921db22753b2e41e29c21cf50d02096. . .
```

Like `docker build`, `docker container create` also outputs a SHA256 hash. This hash uniquely identifies the container that was created. If we were to re-run this exact command, but without the `--name` argument, it would create a second container with a different hash. Without using `--name`, the hash is how you identify containers to other Docker commands (which we, thankfully, will not have to do since we'll be using other tools later on to help bring it all together).

We now have a computer on our desk with a hard drive in it. Let's turn it on.

6.3.4 Starting the Container

To start the container, use `docker container start`:

```
> docker container start catsay-container
catsay-container
```

In production environments, this is typically all you'd do. You'd create the container to run whatever production workload you need to run, e.g. a web server or database. Our dev environment is more like a virtual machine where we will issue commands to it while it sits idle.

6.3.5 Running Commands in the Container

We execute a command inside a running container with `docker container exec`. It accepts the name of a container and then a command to run. We'll run `ruby --version` to check that Ruby was installed (as well as validate our research that the version is Ruby 3.1):

```
> docker container exec catsay-container ruby --version
ruby 3.1.2p20 (2022-04-12 revision 4491bb740a) [aarch64-linu. . .
```

Great! Don't worry about how verbose the command line invocation is—we'll make it better later. For now, let's undo all of this and reset our Docker environment back to how it was.

6.3.6 Stopping a Container so We Can Remove it and then Remove its Image

First is to `docker stop` the container:

```
> docker container stop catsay-container
catsay-container
```

Next, we'll remove the container:

```
> docker container rm catsay-container
catsay-container
```

Lastly, we can remove the image with `docker image rm`:

```
> docker image rm catsay-dev:debian-12.1
Untagged: catsay-dev:debian-12.1
Deleted: sha256:409b9632393c8d1c3caa6efe4601f486fc317bd711e3. . .
```

Note that it "Untagged" the image before deleting it. This is a reminder that image names are really tags and can point to anything. If this image had another tag on it, `docker image rm` would've left the image there, and only removed the tag you gave to `docker image rm`. We'll dig deeper into these nuances in "Managing Your Docker Install" on page 111.

All of this work, from building the Dockerfile, to running a command to cleaning up, is a good demonstration of how our dev environment is going to work. The Dockerfile acts as a manifest of what we need to do development, and the Docker Engine, through the use of containers, allows us to actually develop software.

Next, we need to install NodeJS but, before that, let's learn more about `RUN` by arranging to update Bundler, which manages a Ruby project's dependencies. Bundler's version is managed separately from Ruby itself.

To update Bundler, we'll run `gem install bundler`. Regardless of your familiarity with Ruby, it's a good exercise for you to try to establish a chain of trust for that command. Even though I've known how to update Bundler for years, actually proving to myself that the Bundler team explicitly says this is the way to do it was not as easy as I thought.

We can install it with a new `RUN` directive like so:

```
# Dockerfile.dev

  # From https://www.ruby-lang.org/en/documentation/installatio. . .
  # NOTE: build-essential is needed to install Ruby C extension. . .
  RUN apt-get install --quiet --yes ruby-full build-essential
→ # Hey Reader! Put a url here to prove this is
→ #             the right way to update Bundler :)
→ RUN gem install bundler
```

Now, we'll install NodeJS, which will allow us to understand *layers*.

6.4 Using Layers to Manage Installation

Each `RUN` directive creates what is called a *layer*. This layer can be thought of us a diff against the previous layer (or against the base image for the first `RUN` directive). These layers are cached by Docker and can dramatically speed up image builds. For example, If you created some other Dockerfile that was based on `debian:12.1` and installed Ruby in exactly the same way we are doing it, that image would be built almost instantaneously.

This affects our dev environment because we might be upgrading software on a regular basis. When software is updated, we'd like to minimize the amount of building and installing that has to happen. For example, when a new version of Bundler comes out and we rebuild our image, the system will re-use the cached layer where Ruby itself was installed.

This means that each `RUN` directive must be thoughtfully placed in the right order. Directives have to be ordered based on technical dependencies (upgrading Bundler first requires installing Ruby), but beyond that, you should order `RUN` directives based on frequency of expected change, as shown in Docker Layer Caching on the next page.

Determining the frequency of expected change requires some nuance. Part of the decision involves how often each particular tool is actually updated. For example, chromedriver—which allows you to run browser-based tests using Chrome—changes frequently, but Ruby does not.

Another consideration is the effect a tool has on the stability of your app. CatSay is primarily written in Ruby, so changes to Ruby will have a more drastic effect on it than changes to Node or Bundler. Thus, we likely don't want to change Ruby as

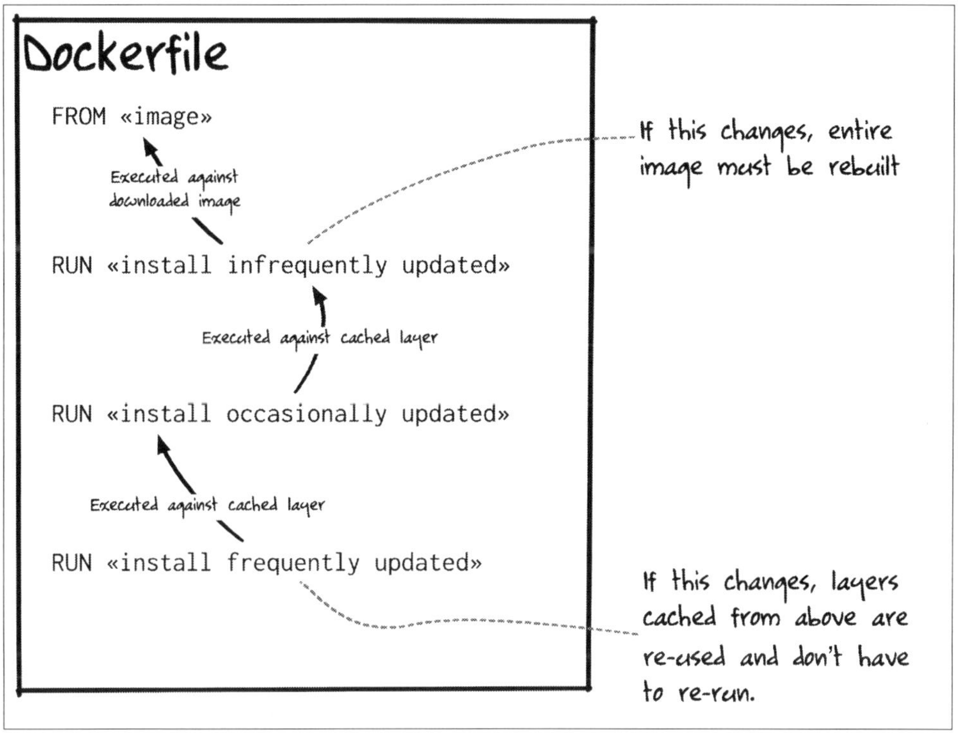

Figure 6.2: Docker Layer Caching

frequently. Way may want to carefully evaluate new releases before adding them to our dev environment.

Given all this, for CatSay, NodeJS is less critical to our app than Ruby, and Bundler is more likely to change than either, so we'll order our Dockerfile with Ruby first, then NodeJS, then Bundler. So, we need to figure out how to install Node.

6.5 Adding Complex Installation Instructions

If you start from `nodejs.org` and follow links to install version 22 (the latest stable version at the time of this writing), you'll end up on `github.com/nodesource`[4], which provides some command-line instructions. At the time of this writing, those instructions are three steps:

1. `curl -fsSL https://deb.nodesource.com/setup_22.x -o node_setup.sh`
2. `bash node_setup.sh`
3. `apt-get install -y nodejs`

If you aren't familiar with how Apt (the name of the software that provides `apt-get`) works, it will install packages from a configured list of package repositories. In the

[4] https://github.com/nodesource/distributions?tab=readme-ov-file#using-debian-as-root-nodejs-22

case of NodeJS, they maintain their own repository, and the script node_setup.sh sets all that up. So, these instructions have you download that script, run it, then use apt-get install.

We know that RUN allows us to run commands in our Docker image as it's being built. We could use these instructions from nodejs.org to create three RUN directives. But, we shouldn't.

6.5.1 Combining Multiple Commands into One Directive

Here's how our Dockerfile would look if we created three RUN directives, one for each command:

```
RUN curl -fsSL https://deb.nodesource.com/setup_22.x -o node_setup.sh
RUN bash node_setup.sh
RUN apt-get install -y nodejs
```

This would result in NodeJS 22 being installed properly. It would create three layers, however: one in which the script node_setup.sh had been downloaded from the Internet, one in which the script has been run, and one in which NodeJS has been installed. There is no real benefit to having these in separate RUN directives, however there *is* a benefit to combining them into one.

Your Dockerfile will be easier to understand and maintain when each layer—each RUN directive—completes a logical, higher level task, such as installing NodeJS. Another way to think about this is that you don't ever want a Docker image that only has half of the setup instructions installed.

Further, separating commands can lead to some hard-to-debug situations. Perhaps the call to curl completed successfully, but something went wrong on Node's side and node_setup.sh is wrong. Installing NodeJS would fail, and re-running docker build would re-use the layer where the node_setup.sh was downloaded, essentially re-using the broken file.

To combine these commands into a single directive, we'll need to learn a bit of Bash symbolese: &&. In "The Arcane World of the UNIX Command Line" on page 63, we'll talk in detail about how commands are executed, which are considered failures, and how to manage that. For now, just know that you can run any number of commands separated by two-ampersands (&&) and all of them will run in order, assuming each one succeeds.

6.5.2 Adding the Node Installation to our Dockerfile

Let's add this to Dockerfile.dev between the install of Ruby and the install of Bundler. Note that we are changing the options given to apt-get install to be their long-form versions since this will make it easier for anyone to understand what it does. Also note the use of backslashes to allow the single command-line to be extend over several lines of text.

```
# Dockerfile.dev

  # From https://www.ruby-lang.org/en/documentation/installatio. . .
  # NOTE: build-essential is needed to install Ruby C extension. . .
  RUN apt-get install --quiet --yes ruby-full build-essential
→
→ # Based on
→ # https://github.com/nodesource/distributions?tab=readme-ov-file
→ # #using-debian-as-root-nodejs-22
→ RUN curl -fsSL https://deb.nodesource.com/setup_22.x -o node_setup.sh && \
→     bash node_setup.sh && \
→     apt-get install --quiet --yes nodejs
  # Hey Reader! Put a url here to prove this is
  #             the right way to update Bundler :)
  RUN gem install bundler
```

This RUN directive has been through four iterations during the time I was writing all this. Of the four versions, two were identical, and the other two were totally different. This is the world of Linux software installation. Each vendor has their own way to do it, and it will change over time. That's why it's important to keep a reference to where you found the commands so you can easily monitor them for changes.

This gives our image five layers, including the base image as shown in the figure "Dev Image Layers" on the next page.

We're almost done, but we need to add a few more things beyond just installing software.

6.6 Adding Configuration to the Dockerfile

There are two things we should add to `Dockerfile.dev` that will help us later on when we set up ancillary services.

The first is to use the `CMD` directive. Thus far, when we've run `docker container create`, we had to supply the command `sleep infinity` to keep the container running. If we omitted that, Docker will use the Dockerfile's `CMD` value. So, we'll set that directly in `Dockerfile.dev`. That way, our use of `docker container create` will be simpler (later, when we automate this with Docker Compose, it'll be one less thing to specify).

The second is to use the directive `WORKDIR` which will help us when we mount the source code into the container. `WORKDIR` essentially sets the current directory for any `RUN` directive after it. Any `docker container exec` invocation will run relative to the last `WORKDIR` directive in the Dockerfile. `WORKDIR` will *also* create the directory for us.

Here's all the changes:

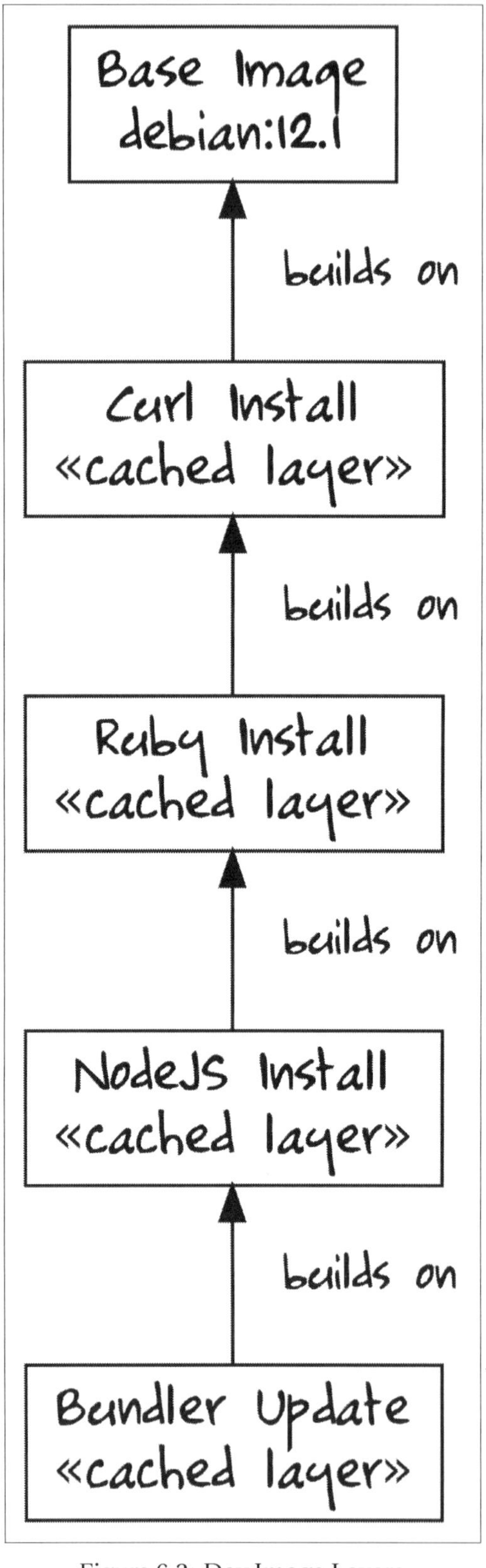

Figure 6.3: Dev Image Layers

```
# Dockerfile.dev

  # Hey Reader! Put a url here to prove this is
  #             the right way to update Bundler :)
  RUN gem install bundler
→
→ # Source code will be available here
→ WORKDIR /root/catsay
→
→ # Stay busy when we start so we can run commands
→ CMD sleep infinity
```

Note that each directive has a comment preceding it to explain why it's there. Always do this. You may forget or your team members may not be able to figure it out. If you are working with some agile coach that says code should be self-documenting, you will need to sneak these comments past their review. Those agile coaches *hate* comments[5].

Now, let's build the image to make sure it is all working:

```
> docker build --quiet --file Dockerfile.dev --tag  \
  catsay-dev:debian-12.1 .
«lots of output»
```

This looks great. Next, we need to learn how to create and start a container that can access our source code as we edit it, as well as expose the right ports needed for local development.

[5]I'm sure it has nothing to do with ensuring a continued need for their services.

7

Publishing Ports and Mounting Volumes to Do Development

If you want to develop software, don't drum up the people to write code, structure the app, and close JIRA tickets. Instead, teach them to yearn for the vast and endless frustration of debugging networking and hardware issues.

—*Antoine de St. Exupery (apocryphal)*

As mentioned in the last chapter, a Docker container won't allow any of its ports to be accessed from the outside world. This makes good sense as a default, but if we are building a web app, we're gonna need to access our app through a browser. Fortunately, Docker allows mapping ports from a container to your computer via *publishing*.

We also haven't talked about how the container gets access to the source code. We want to be able to run our own editor on our own computer, editing the source code like normal, while the app running in the container can see those changes. We can do that with a type of a volume called a *bind mount*.

7.1 One Does Not Map a Port... One Publishes It

Mapping ports in Docker is surprisingly convoluted, especially given how terse the syntax is. As mentioned, CatSay runs on port 3000. For the sake of learning, we're going to map that to port 4242 on the host (i.e. your computer).

To publish a port, we'll use the `--publish` argument to `docker container create`. The syntax is laudable for both its terseness and counter-intuitiveness.

```
--publish «host port»:«port in container to publish»
```

Perhaps it's just me, but semantically, we are publishing a port inside a container to a port on the host, and in my mind that means the arguments should be reversed. Anyway.

When we create our container, we'll add `--publish 4242:3000` to the command line. Let's not create that container just yet, because we need the source code so we can run the app and make this configuration useful.

7.2 Mounting A Bind Mount

Docker volumes are disks, and what we want is to have our Docker container be able to access a disk that contains CatSay's source code. But we don't want it to just have a copy, we want it to have a live view, so that when we make changes using our editor of choice[1], those changes are reflected in the container.

How do we mount volumes? The first problem you'll run into is that sometimes Docker instructions use the word *mount* to mean a volume and sometimes they use it to mean a specific type of volume. It can be confusing.

There are three types of volumes: volume(!), tmpfs, and bind. We want *bind*, which says it is[2] "a file or directory on the host machine [that] is mounted into a container". Remember, "host" is your computer, so this sounds right.

If you run `docker container create --help`, you'll see two potential options for setting this up: `-v` and `--mount`. So, do we use `-v` (which "bind mounts a volume", whatever that means) or `--mount` (which "attach[es] a filesystem mount to the container")?

The answer is that both do *almost* the same thing but with a different syntax. `-v` uses a horrible colon-delimited terse thing that I strongly recommend you never use because it will be confusing and save you exactly no time. But it will create the destination directory for you.

Instead, we'll use `--mount`, which accepts a comma-delimited set of key/value pairs, but does *not* create the destination directory for you (this is why we used `WORKDIR` to create it in the `Dockerfile.dev`). Who is to say why this differs from `-v`? Not me.

The keys for `--mount` are somewhat documented in Docker's official docs[3], and here is what we'll use for each:

- `type` is, as mentioned, `bind`
- `source` is not really documented on the volumes page. On the bind mounts page, it tells us that it's the path to the directory we want to share from our computer.
- `destination` is the directory where the volume will be accessible inside the container. We'll use the value for `WORKDIR` in our `Dockerfile.dev`: `/root/catsay`
- `readonly` we should omit because we want this to be read/write.
- `volume-opts` is not documented at all, so I hope we don't need it!

The value for `source` must be the full path to wherever your source code is—it can't be a relative path. Given that `pwd` will print out the current working directory, you can put `$(pwd)` into the option so the full path is automatically calculated.

This means that our `--mount` option will look like so:

[1] Which should be vim
[2] https://docs.docker.com/storage/bind-mounts/
[3] https://docs.docker.com/storage/volumes/#choose-the--v-or---mount-flag

```
--mount type=bind,source=$(pwd),target=/root/catsay
```

With our port set up, let's create our container (note that I had to use \ to spread this command over multiple lines—that will work for you but you can also omit the \ and type it all on one line).

```
> docker container create --name catsay-container --publish  \
  4242:3000 --mount  \
  type=bind,source=$(pwd),target=/root/catsay  \
  catsay-dev:debian-12.1
6105cc0adf42c2781c2333d3903192c22c0fdb831698d0de70c3656c316a. . .
```

Windows Network Access

If you are using Windows Subsystem for Linux, the first time you run a command like this, you will be asked to allow Docker for network access. You will need to choose whatever option allows such access.

Start it up:

```
> docker container start catsay-container
catsay-container
```

Remember, because we specified `CMD`, the container should be dutifully running `sleep infinity`.

CatSay's README says we should run `bin/setup`, so let's do that using `docker container exec`:

```
> docker container exec catsay-container bin/setup
«lots of output»
```

`bin/setup` produces a lot of output, but you should see some help text at the end of it, if everything went well. This text (along with the README) documents `bin/run` as the way to run the app. Before we try that, we have to take a short digression into UNIX arcana. If we were to run `docker container exec catsay-container bin/run`, `bin/run` would start up and serve up the CatSay app. But, if we hit Ctrl-C to stop `bin/run`, it would only stop `docker container exec` and `bin/run` would remain running inside the container.

After we script everything, this detail won't matter, but it matters now, so let's learn a bit about UNIX. `docker container exec` uses what is called a *non-interactive* shell, and it *does not allocate a TTY*. Defining these terms precisely is not easy. Docker's docs don't even try.

Let me explain. No, there is too much. Let me sum up. An interactive shell allows you to interact with the command that `docker container exec` executed, and a

TTY is the name for a terminal emulator which is required to allow the command to receive Ctrl-C.

Thus, we will override the defaults by using `--interactive` and `--tty`. These can be shortened to `-it` which you may have seen from many blog posts about Docker.

If you run the command below, you should be able to see CatSay in all its glory on `localhost:4242`, as in the screenshot "CatSay Homepage" below.

```
docker container exec --interactive --tty catsay-container bin/run
```

Figure 7.1: CatSay Homepage

Nice! Now, let's see a basic dev workflow.

7.3 Adding a Feature Using our Dev Environment

Suppose you are the lead developer on CatSay. Chris from marketing comes running over to your desk in an absolute frenzy. Chris has discovered that the competitor to CatSay, CatsTalk, has trademarked the phrase "The Website That Makes Cats Say Things", which is what CatSay is using as its subtitle. We have to change this ASAP or face the lawyers!

Open up `app/views/index.html.erb` and fix this pending legal issue. Chris and his team were up all night workshopping a new phrase, which is "Request That Cats Verbalize Words". While they get it through the trademark office, it's up to you to update the app.

```
<%# app/views/index.html.erb %>

    <body class="ff-sans">
      <header class="pa-3 bg-black white">
        <h1 class="f-6 ma-0 ff-fantasy mv-1">CatSay</h1>
→       <h2 class="f-5 ma-0 ff-fantasy mv-1">
→         Request That Cats Verbalize Words&trade;
→       </h2>
      </header>
      <main>
        <section data-testid="stairs" class="<%= @pic == 'stair. . .
```

You'll need to stop the server and restart it. Wherever you have `docker container exec catsay-container bin/run` running, hit Ctrl-C to stop it, then re-run it (CatSay is not set up to auto-reload itself on code changes). Note that this is *not* restarting Docker or the container we have built—it's just restarting the app we're running inside it.

You should now see the lawsuit-avoiding version of the site at `localhost:4242`, as in the screenshot "CatSay Homepage Updated" below.

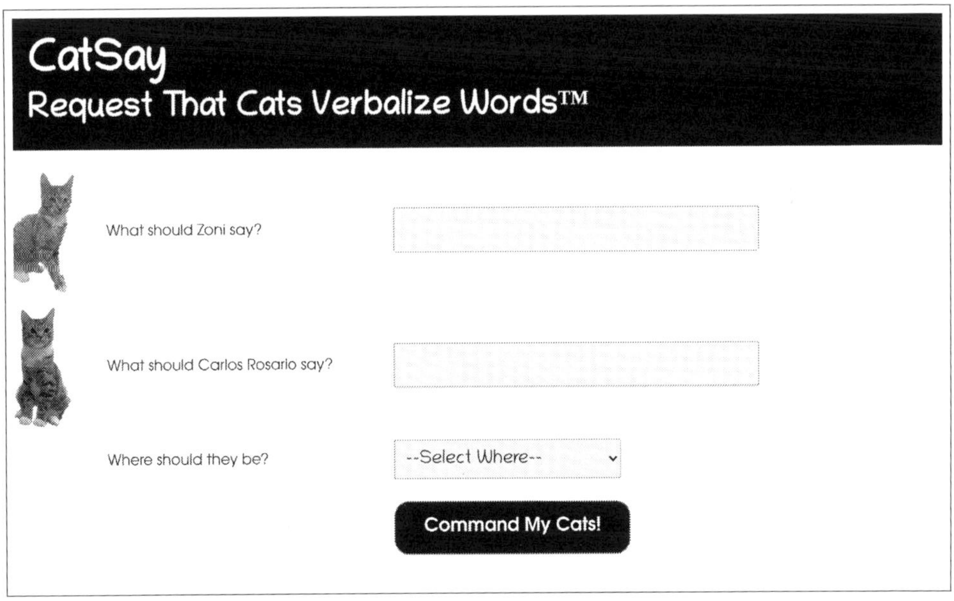

Figure 7.2: CatSay Homepage Updated

Crisis averted!

We now have the tools to perform all the same workflows we have when running code natively, *except* the ability to run ancillary services like databases. That's next.

8

Running Databases and Caches with One Line of Code

It was actually, it was beyond belief. These were first and original lines of YAML, but the Git history showed no corrections of any kind. Not one. He had simply written down configuration already finished! Line after line of it as if he were just pasting from Stack Overflow. And YAML, finished as no YAML is ever finished. Displace one space and there would be diminishment. Displace one colon and the structure would fall. It was clear to me that infrastructure I had seen in the Archbishop's palace had been no accident. Here again was the very Voice of Bob! I was staring through the cage of those meticulous keystrokes at an absolute beauty.

—Tony Salieri, Amadeus Ex Machina

The README of CatSay indicates that if it can connect to Redis, it provides additional functionality. Redis is a key/value database that is often used as a cache. This is precisely the sort of service we don't want to have to figure out how to install on our computer or otherwise deal with.

Remember when we ran `uname -a` inside the container configured with the Debian image? There are other images on Docker Hub that are configured to run software and not just an operating system. In fact, Docker Hub's vast collection of pre-made images is a big reason why it's a good tool to build our dev environment with.

What we need is a trusted image that runs Redis. If we can identify that, we can use the skills we've learned to run it with one line of code. But, we can do even better.

We can use *Docker Compose* to run Redis alongside our dev container, network them together, and get a self-contained system of services, all based on a pretty short configuration file. Granted, that file is in YAML, but it's still going to be a net win.

First, let's establish yet another chain of trust to locate the Redis image to run.

8.1 Establishing a Chain of Trust for Images

To establish a chain of trust of an image to run Redis, we'll use the same process we learned about in Finding Images You Can Trust on page 23. We'll start on Redis' website, `redis.io`[1].

From there, click "Download", then "More installation options", then "Go to Redis DockerHub". This will lead you to DockerHub's page for Redis at `hub.docker.com/_/redis`. If you scroll way down to the section titled "Image Variants", you can see that these images use tags the same way Debian's images do. Again, this convention is entirely up to the vendor, and not explicitly supported by any of Docker's tooling.

You'll also note that the documentation mentions Alpine Linux and that it's possible to use an image with Redis running on that, instead of Debian (which is the default in this case). As a demonstration of the flexibility our dev environment offers, let's use the Alpine-based version. There's no requirement to use the same Linux distribution to run our app and Redis. Thus, we'll use `7-2-alpine` as the tag.

That said, you want to choose the OS in the same way you chose your base image's OS: are there technical requirements, what are you running in production, and what is your computer's processor architecture?

Before we move on, there's one other thing to note about establishing a chain of trust and the management of images on DockerHub.

8.2 Understanding Who Maintains an Image

If you go back to the Debian page on DockerHub (at `hub.docker.com/_/debian`), you'll see that it says "Maintained by Debian Developers tianon and paultag". There is also a note that says "Docker Official Image". Now, look at the Redis page on DockerHub.

While Redis' page also has the "Docker Official image" note on it, it says it is "Maintained by the Docker Community". If you click that link, you'll end up at the "Docker Library" GitHub organization at `github.com/docker-library`. Unfortunately, there is no way to validate that this GitHub organization is any particular person or even associated with Docker.

But, as we mentioned in Finding Images You Can Trust on the next page, we have to assume Docker Hub is not compromised, and that "the Docker Community" is actually Docker.

I'm pointing this out because you may find images that are maintained by Docker, marked as official, but aren't linked from the vendor's website[2]. For development, you can generally trust images like this. Docker has a page on their documentation site[3] that explains more details about this process. It's too bad that they don't

---

[1] https://redis.io

[2] In an early draft of this book, Redis had no such link, instead linking to the latest tagged version of some other product they offer.

[3] https://docs.docker.com/trusted-content/official-images/

bring it all together more clearly from the various pages, but generally everything is trustworthy[4].

OK, back to Redis, we are going to use the image named `redis:7-2-alpine`. With what we've learned so far, we could certain create a Docker container that uses that as an image. And, while we could publish Redis' ports so that CatSay could access it, this will get tiresome and complicated.

Instead, we can do this much more easily with *Docker Compose.*

8.3 Docker Compose Configures a Virtual Network

See the figure "Docker Network Dev Environment" on page 51 for an overview of what we are going to create. We already have the know-how to publish our app's port, connect it to our browser, and set up a bind mount so we can edit code that the dev environment can see. We'll now set up the rest of what's in that diagram.

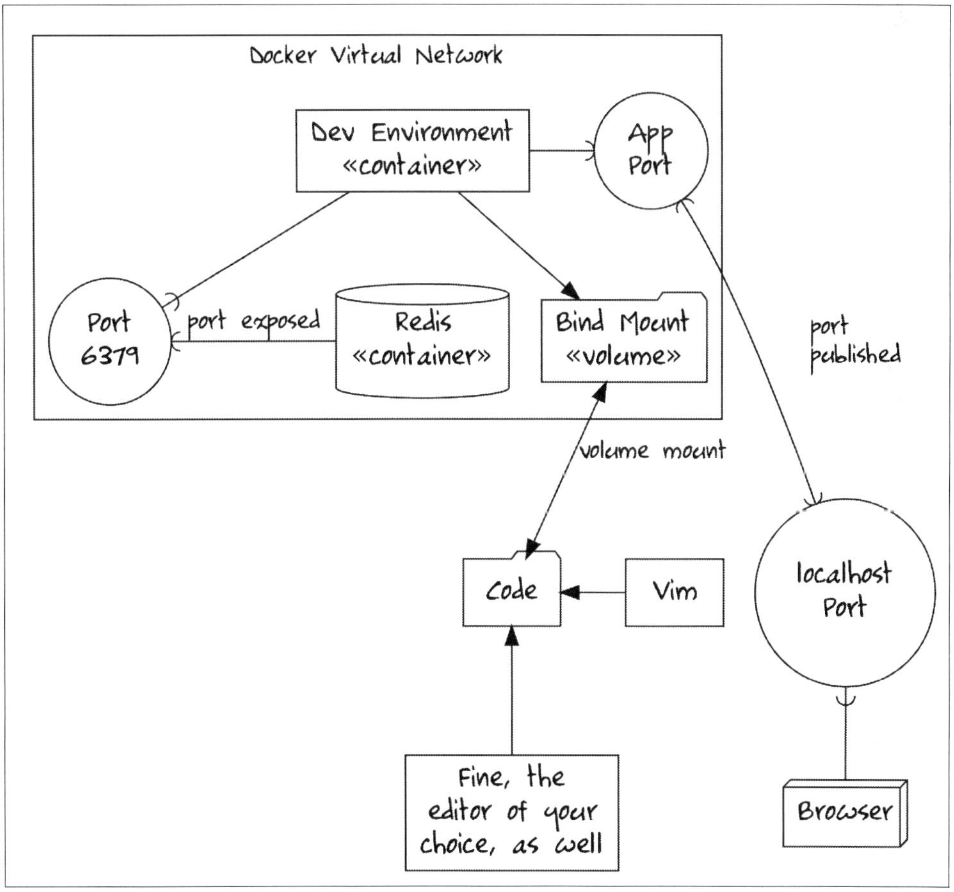

Figure 8.1: Docker Network Dev Environment

[4]Though, still, I would have a hard time trusting *any* of this for production workloads as it feels like a house of cards.

Docker Compose is a feature of Docker that allows us to create a network of images, running together and starting/stopping as one. The *compose file* (which, sadly, is YAML[5]), allows us to list several services that will all be able to see each other on a virtual private network, replete with unique hostnames that can't be accessed outside your computer.

Docker Compose's YAML file *also* allows us to specify several configuration options that we've been using on the command-line, thus improving our workflow substantially. And, it's all brought together via `docker compose`, so we can start and stop all these containers with one command.

Let's create one to see what it looks like. We'll put it in `docker-compose.dev.yml` (again, to indicate the purpose of this file). The stanza under `app:` is where the configuration that replaces the command-line arguments goes, and should hopefully look familiar. Note that since this is a file and not a command-line invocation, our use of `$(pwd)` for the bind mount's `source` won't work. Fortunately, this configuration option can be a relative path from the location of the compose file (which is not possible by using the command line). Thus, it can be `"."`.

```
# docker-compose.dev.yml

services:
  app:
    image: catsay-dev:debian-12.1
    init: true
    volumes:
      - type: bind
        source: "."
        target: "/root/catsay"
    ports:
      - "4242:3000"
  redis:
    image: redis:7.2-alpine
```

The only new thing is `init: true`. Without it, the command we specified in the Dockerfile will be the only command running and this creates a potentially odd situation in the container. The most observable result is that shutting down the containers is very slow. `init: true` instructs Docker to run a command that runs our command. For whatever reason, this causes shutdown to be very fast.

Each key under `services` will be the hostname used to access whatever ports are exposed or published. `app:` is just a convention I use to mean "the app being developed", but it can be anything, as long as it is a valid hostname.

[5]If you've somehow managed to avoid using YAML, I strongly recommend you avoid fancy or complex things. You should also quote everything because, depending on the context, the country code for Norway could be interpreted as the boolean `false`. I wish I were kidding.

The `redis:` stanza is a bit different. The key, again, can be anything, but all we need to specify inside it is the image name. Note that if the app required *two* Redises (say one for caching and one for background jobs), you'd add a third stanza, and would use different names, but the same image:

```
services:
  app:
    # ..
  redis-cache:
    image: redis:7.2-alpine
  redis-jobs:
    image: redis:7.2-alpine
```

This is where the image/container distinction is important. This configuration would result in two containers running the same image. But, since they'd be used to run different containers, they would not share any storage with each other. Anything put into the Redis running inside `redis-cache` would **not** be accessible to the Redis running in `redis-jobs`.

Given this configuration—or lack thereof—what exactly happens when we start a container using the `redis:7.2-alpine` image? How do we know that this actually runs Redis?

8.4 Understanding What an Image You Found ~~in a Parking Lot~~ On Docker Hub Will Do When You Use It

We saw that the `CMD` directive allowed our Dockerfile to specify what command to run when `docker container start` is executed.
Since Redis' `Dockerfile` is open source, we can inspect it to see what it does. At the time of this writing, that file is available on GitHub[6]. If you examine it, you'll that `CMD` is set to run `redis-server`, which certainly sounds like it runs Redis. You'll also see some new directives near it (toward the end of the file):

```
→ COPY docker-entrypoint.sh /usr/local/bin/
→ ENTRYPOINT ["docker-entrypoint.sh"]

→ EXPOSE 6379
  CMD ["redis-server"]
```

The first is `COPY`. This directive tells Docker to copy a file from the machine where the image was built into the image. This is slightly terrifying because it means

[6]https://github.com/docker-library/redis/blob/9b538c33746872dcd1e8c809cbde9f21ac2ec3ac/7.2/alpine/Dockerfile

the image could have literally anything in it. You can reasonably assume the files come from the same repository, so for example the file `docker-entrypoint.sh`[7] is copied and used as the `ENTRYPOINT` later.

`ENTRYPOINT` is a way to customize how `CMD` (or whatever is given to `docker container start` and `docker container exec`) is executed. The default is a shell, like `bin/sh` or `bin/bash`, and this means that `CMD` is... executed in a shell.

It's not common to need to modify this, but depending on what has to be run, it can be useful. Redis needed to override it, so the effect of starting a container with this image is that instead of `bin/sh redis-server` being run, Docker will run `docker-entrypoint.sh redis-server`. If you `docker container exec` any command, like `redis-cli`, Docker will actually execute `docker-entrypoint.sh redis-cli`.

The last directive to point out is `EXPOSE`. This is how a port is exposed from whatever is running in the container. If you recall, an *exposed* port is not necessarily published. It's available to other containers in the same network, but not from the Docker host i.e. your computer. In the case of Redis, port 6379 is exposed—that's the default port Redis runs on. Our app will be able to see it, but our computer will not be able to.

The reason for this digression into the Dockerfile and these directives is that you often don't get great documentation about what the image is going to do or how to consume the services it wraps. Some light spelunking into the Dockerfile can help figure that out.

Let's try running everything, next.

8.5 Docker Compose Can Replace Most Other Commands

`docker compose up` will create and start up all the containers for each service using the configured images, hence "up". This will do the equivalent of `docker container create` and `docker container start` for us.

Let's try it now, using `--file` to specify our compose file (which is only required because we did *not* name our file `docker-compose.yml`). We're also going to use *detached mode* which will allow it to run in the background while we execute commands in the same terminal.

Note that I'm adding `--ansi=never` and `--no-color` to avoid creating unprintable characters for the book. You can omit those and enjoy the 8-color animations the team was working on instead of re-thinking the concept of "latest".

```
> docker compose --ansi=never --file docker-compose.dev.yml up  \
   --detach --no-color
 Network catsay_default  Creating
 Network catsay_default  Created
 Container catsay-app-1  Creating
```

[7] https://github.com/docker-library/redis/blob/9b538c33746872dcd1e8c809cbde9f21ac2ec3ac/7.2/alpine/docker-entrypoint.sh

```
Container catsay-redis-1  Creating
Container catsay-app-1  Created
Container catsay-redis-1  Created
Container catsay-app-1  Starting
Container catsay-redis-1  Starting
Container catsay-app-1  Started
Container catsay-redis-1  Started
```

Instead of `docker container exec`, we can use `docker compose exec` to run commands inside a container. `docker compose exec` uses the *service* name from the YAML file, so we don't have to mess around with giving containers names. `docker compose exec` also defaults to using an interactive shell with a TTY, so we don't need to worry about stuff like `--interactive` or `--tty`.

Since we've restarted everything, there is a chance that anything we did inside the previous container is gone, since the storage is ephemeral. This means that any RubyGems or Node modules installed by `bin/setup` may no longer be inside the container. Note the use of the word "may".

Back in "Build and Testing and Image" on page 33, we ran `docker container start` and used a named container. If that container didn't exist, the command would fail. If the container *did* exist, it would be started and be in the same state it was when it was exited—including any bytes written to its internal (virtual) disk.

Thus, if we started that container, ran `bin/setup`, stopped, and then *restarted* it, the results of `bin/setup` would still be there. All RubyGems and Node modules installed before would still be installed. But our `docker compose` based setup doesn't provide this level of control.

If the container that was used the first time we ran `bin/setup` is gone, the command we just ran—`docker compose up`—will create a new container from the image. That container *won't* contain our RubyGems and Node modules. Whew!

I don't know about you, but I don't like having to think about stuff like this unless it's necessary. Just as `if` statements tend to breed complexity in our software, so do they complicate our workflows. The way I deal with not knowing if the old container is still around is to run `bin/setup` again every time I restart everything. I design `bin/setup` to be idempotent so that if it doesn't need to install anything, it runs quickly.

The other option is to *not* do this and see if your app breaks, then run `bin/setup` if it does. I'll be honest, I do that, too, because I forget. Anyway, let's be safe and run `bin/setup` again now. I do want to stress that this is only needed when you restart the *Foundational Layer*. You are likely to keep this running all day or even all week, so you should not need to bootstrap your app's dev environment very often.

```
> docker compose --ansi=never --file docker-compose.dev.yml  \
  exec app bin/setup
«lots of output»
```

Now use docker compose exec to do bin/run and see that the app is (still) available at localhost:4242, as in the screenshot "CatSay Homepage With Redis" on the next page.

```
> docker compose --ansi=never --file docker-compose.dev.yml exec app bin/run
```

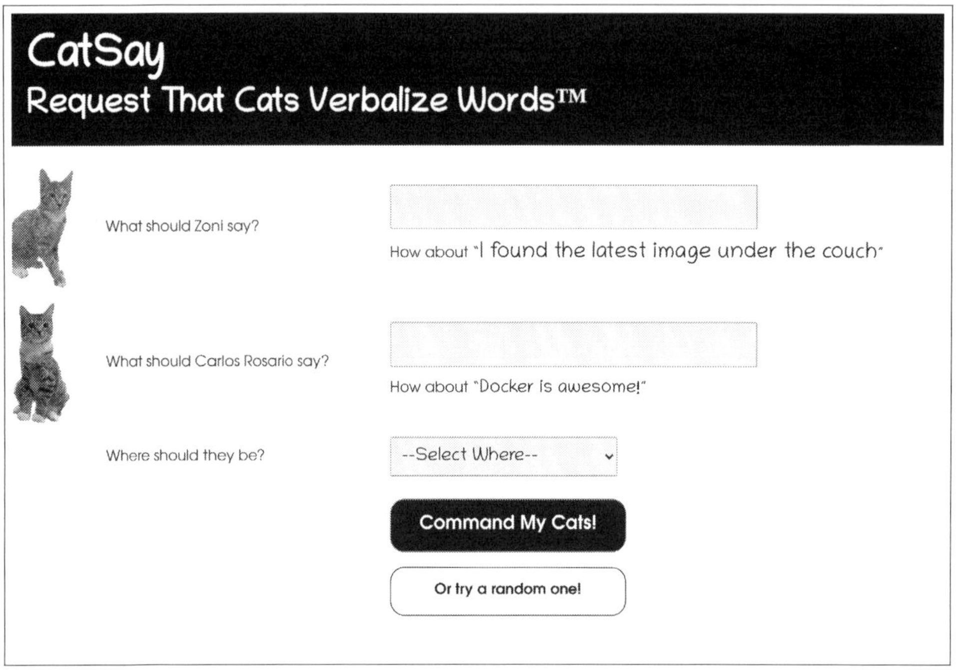

Figure 8.2: CatSay Homepage With Redis

Note that the app is behaving differently because it now has access to Redis. bin/setup seeded Redis with some example things the cats could say. You are free to use them or have it choose a random one for you.

Once you are done, everything can be shut down with docker compose down.

```
> docker compose --ansi=never --file docker-compose.dev.yml  \
  down
 Container catsay-app-1  Stopping
 Container catsay-redis-1  Stopping
 Container catsay-redis-1  Stopped
 Container catsay-redis-1  Removing
 Container catsay-redis-1  Removed
 Container catsay-app-1  Stopped
 Container catsay-app-1  Removing
 Container catsay-app-1  Removed
 Network catsay_default  Removing
 Network catsay_default  Removed
```

This workflow is not bad. Keeping in mind that we still have yet more room for improvement, this is what's needed by any developer to be able to work on this app (or any app):

1. Clone the repo
2. Run `docker build --file Dockerfile.dev --tag catsay-dev:debian-12.1`
3. Run `docker compose up`
4. Use `docker compose exec app «command»` to do development

In a documentation-based dev environment, steps 2 and 3 would be replaced by a potentially lengthy set of manual instructions. In a non-virtualized environment, step 3 would either be an incredibly complex automation script, or yet more documentation. Despite the verbosity of these commands, the Docker version we have created is better.

But we can make it even better still.

9

What is a Good User Experience for Automation Scripts?

In the beginning when Ada created the operating system, it was a formless void and darkness covered the face of the front-side bus. A wind swept over the file system. Ada said "Let there be Bash" and there was Bash. And Ada saw that Bash was, well, OK for now.

—*North Sea Scrolls, translation debated*

If a developer asked me what programming languages would serve them throughout their entire career, I would say, in order: SQL, JavaScript, and Bash[1].

Bash is everywhere. Linux operating systems all have it. macOS has it. Even Windows—when you set up the Windows Subsystem for Linux—has it. Bash is also pretty stable. A script written 10 years ago will probably still work the same now as it did then. This means that, despite its often confusing syntax, Bash is a great choice for dev environment automation.

9.1 Bash's Ubiquity Outweighs your Favorite Programming Language

I'll be honest, I don't enjoy writing Bash scripts. I want to minimize the time I spend writing Bash and the amount of Bash code I am responsible for. It *is* a strange language with strange behaviors. So why not use Ruby? Or Python, or whatever *your* preferred language is?

The reason is the particular nature of automating a dev environment. By definition, this automation must work and succeed before any developer tools have been installed. Sure, my Mac has Ruby, but what version? And is that version compatible with whatever version is on your Linux box? Probably not.

In the degenerate environment of a fresh developer workstation, Bash is the only thing that can be relied-upon to be there. And, because Bash *is* stable, and hasn't

[1] Regular Expressions are a close fourth, but there's a part of me that hopes for a very bright future in which developers don't have to learn them.

had many breaking changes over the years, you can expect that a Bash script that works on Windows Subsystem for Linux will work on a Mac and on any bona fide Linux[2].

9.2 Despite It's Flaws, You Can Make a Good UI with Bash

It's not controversial to state that it's easier to make a good user experience in a language like Ruby or JavaScript than compared to Bash. Bash is not easy to use, and I won't claim it's remotely fun. Some of that is by its nature, but I find a big chunk of the difficulty with Bash is lack of familiarity. We'll change that over the course of the next few chapters.

As we'll see, by applying some care and rigor to some newfound knowledge, Bash *can* be used to make a great user experience. This is especially true of the problem at hand: automating our dev environment.

The scripts we will write are just that: scripts. They are ultimately automating a few straightforward steps that would otherwise require a lot of fussy command line options and verbose invocations. We don't have to account for a lot of variables.

Here are the tenets of user experience we want in our dev environment automation:

1. No command should require an argument to do the right thing.
2. Every command should respond to `-h` by producing a detailed help message about what it does and how to use it.
3. Commands should output what they are doing, so that their behavior can be understood.
4. Commands should verify any assumption they make, and provide a useful error message to the user when assumptions are invalid.

Bash is eminently capable of these things.

To be specific, we need to automate building the docker image, starting/stopping the dev environment, and executing commands inside it. To do that, we'll create four scripts as outlined in the following table:

Table 9.1: Automation Scripts

Script	Purpose
`build`	Build the Docker image
`start`	Start the dev environment
`stop`	Stop the dev environment
`exec`	Execute a command in the dev environment

[2]If you've used the Heroku CLI anytime in the last 10 years, you will have seen that it basically embedded an entire programming language runtime into the package. First it was done in Ruby, then later in JavaScript. That's the only way they could ensure the CLI worked when installed on an unknown computer.

We aren't going to put this in a directory called `bin` (which would be the conventional UNIX-like place for such things). The reason is that our app may have its own scripts in `bin` and it will be less confusing if we keep them separate from the dev environment. While a directory named `dev-environment` has the virtue of being explicit, we don't want to have to type that out, or even autocomplete it.

Our scripts will go in a directory called `dx`, which is a common abbreviation for "Developer Experience". That way, anything in `dx` can be understood to manage the dev environment, and `bin/` can serve whatever function our app needs.

Let's make `dx` now:

```
> mkdir -p dx
```

It may seem obvious that you can put `docker build` into `build`, `docker compose up` into `start`, and `docker compose exec` into `exec`, so are we really going to spend several chapters making single-line scripts? Yes and no. These scripts *will* be more robust than just calling one line of code, but they also serve as *protocols*.

9.3 Scripts as Protocols for Future Enhancements

The dev environment we've designed thus far—and will refine over the next few chapters—is relatively simple. We really don't need much more than a simple Dockerfile and a few commands wrapped in a nice UI. But this may not always be the case. Any app that exists for years builds up complexity, and a lot of that complexity shows up in the dev environment setup.

By creating a handful of scripts, we establish *seams* in the workflow and process of managing the dev environment. I like to think of these as a *protocol* that any app conforms to. Every app has a `build` script to set up its Foundational Core. But that script can contain anything. It can be as simple as running `docker build` to as complex as generating a Dockerfile, bootstrapping configuration, and tweaking complex parameters.

But to the developers of the app, it's just a script they run that does the right thing. Whatever the app's needs are over time, they can find a place to be automated in one of our scripts.

Our job in building the first version of the scripts is to keep them simple, but also make it clear where and how they are to be enhanced over time. We'll do this not by trying to guess what our needs will be, but by writing fault-tolerant code that's well-factored and easy to follow, even if you haven't looked at it in a few months.

Let's start by creating a single script that meets all of our needs. We'll use that as a template for the other scripts, which will then allow us to refactor them into something sustainable.

Before all that, we need to learn some basic command line and Bash terminology, since our scripts are going to do things like check for errors, output information, and manage processes.

10

The Arcane World of the UNIX Command Line

If you know the command line and you know yourself, you need not fear the result of a hundred terminal sessions. If you know yourself but not the command line, for every program executed, you will also suffer a core dump. If you know neither the command line nor yourself, you may live a happy, if ignorant, life. I would envy you.

—Sun Tzu, The Art of War, Berkeley translation (discredited)

When you type commands on the command line, you are typing a shell script, one line at a time. This is useful context to have when writing a shell script in a file, because it's partly like programming in a more conventional language, and partly scripting stuff you type on the command line.

There are some conventions and behaviors around all this that you'll need to know. This section may be remedial if you have a lot of experience using the UNIX command line. But, if you don't, it can be extremely confusing and hard to figure out. That's what we'll try to avoid here.

The first thing to understand is how commands are located in the first place.

10.1 The Path is Where Commands are Found

When you type `docker`, how does the shell know what you mean? It knows because of the *path*. Type `echo $PATH` and hit return. You'll see a colon-delimited list of paths.

```
> echo $PATH
/usr/local/bundle/bin:/usr/local/sbin:/usr/local/bin:/usr/sb. . .
```

Each of these contains executables. When you type a command on the command-line and hit return, the shell will look for that command in one of the paths in your, uh, path. If it can't find it, you'll get a probably familiar message like "command not found".

Once a command is located and executed, what happens? There are two important outputs of a command. One is a code indicating if it was successful. The other, which you are more familiar with, is output to the terminal.

10.2 Output Streams Give Control Over Output

When you see output to the terminal, you are actually seeing the combination of two separate streams of output. These two streams are called the *standard output* and the *standard error*. Although they are intermixed by default, as in the diagram below on page 64, they can be separated.

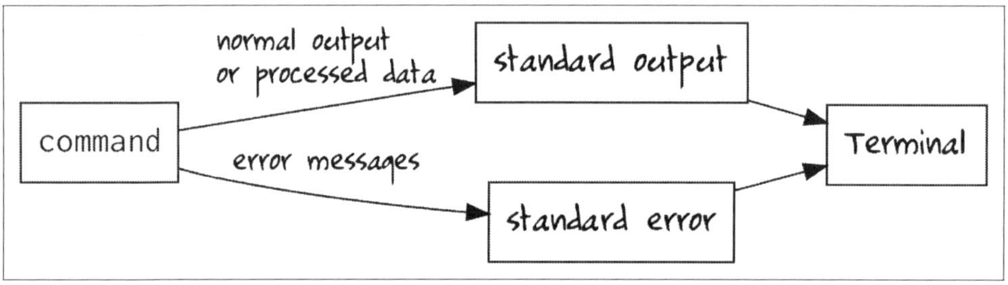

Figure 10.1: Crossing the Output Streams

10.2.1 Two Standard Streams for Output

The purpose of having two streams is to give you control over messages. By convention, error messages appear on the standard error, and all other messages appear on the standard output. Consider `grep`, which searches files for strings. If you run `grep gem Gemfile`, you'll see each line from `Gemfile` that contains the string "gem" on the standard output. If you ran `grep gem blah`, you'll get an error message on the standard error.

The streams can be redirected, for example into files. Run this command:

```
grep gem Gemfile > output1.txt
```

That greater-than sign is telling Bash to redirect the standard output into the file named `output1.txt`. When you run this command, you won't see any output. But, if you examine `output1.txt`, you'll see each line from `Gemfile` that contains the string "gem".

Now try this:

```
grep gem blah > output2.txt
```

You will see an error message printed to the terminal. This is because that error message was printed to the standard error, and the greater-than sign only redirects the standard output. `output2.txt` should be empty, since there wasn't any other output.

Here is where Bash's idiosyncrasies start to show up. Try running this command:

```
grep gem blah 2> output3.txt
```

That's not a typo, you should type the number 2 before that greater-than sign. What this does is tell Bash to redirect the standard *error* into the file. When you run *this* command, you won't see any output, and `output3.txt` will contain the error messages. If you run this:

```
grep gem Gemfile 2> output4.txt
```

You will see the matching lines output to the terminal, because the standard output was not redirected. `output4.txt` will be empty, since there was no standard error output generated by `grep`.

The "2" is the name of a *file descriptor*. In UNIX programming, files are represented by numbers, and "2" is always the standard error. The standard output is "1", and is the assumed file descriptor for redirects. Thus, the invocation `grep gem Gemfile 1> output1.txt` is the same as if we had omitted the "1".

Yes, this is super arcane. But it does kinda, sorta make sense. One thing to know is that these streams can be sent to other commands instead of files.

10.2.2 Redirecting Output to the Input of a Command

When we installed NodeJS, we saw this:

```
curl -fsSL https://deb.nodesource.com/setup_22.x -o node_setup.sh
bash node_setup.sh
```

A previous mechanism to do this avoided the need for a separate script. Without `-o node_setup.sh`, `curl` will output the URL it's asked to fetch to the standard output. Bash can be asked to read commands from what is called the *standard input* (which is a file descriptor numbered 0). When you type commands into bash, you are typing them into the standard input.

To get information from somewhere other than a person typing at a keyboard, the pipe operator (`|`) can be used to connect standard output to input, like so:

```
curl -fsSL https://deb.nodesource.com/setup_22.x | bash -
```

Note the trailing `-`. This tells Bash that it is OK to read commands being piped into it. The entire invocation is often referred to as a *pipeline*.

10.2.3 Redirecting Output to Oblivion AKA `/dev/null`

One last thing about redirecting output is `/dev/null`. `/dev/null` is a type of file that discards whatever is written to it. Because it's a type of file, you'd use `>` or `2>` to send information to it so it could be effectively thrown away without seeing it.

You may have seen commands do this, or even seen something like this:

```
> grep gem Gemfile > /dev/null 2>&1
```

That `2>&1` is saying to combine file descriptor 2 with file descriptor 1. Since the greater-than sign is redirecting the standard output, which is file descriptor 1, the use of `2>&1` means "send the standard error to `/dev/null` also", since "2" is the file descriptor for the standard error.

Is this arcane enough for you? My head hurts thinking about this sometimes, but if you aren't used to this yet, you will get used to it, I promise. You can see a visual overview in the figure "So Many Streams" on page 66.

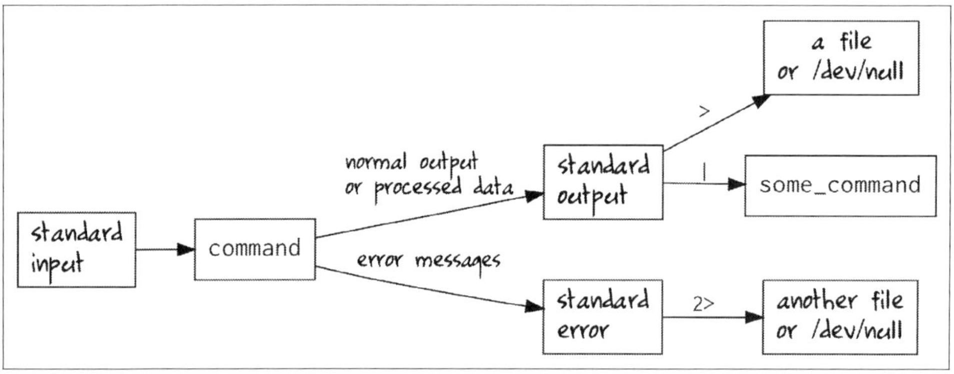

Figure 10.2: So Many Streams

Now, with all this redirecting of output to files, commands, or `/dev/null`, we aren't seeing the output in the terminal. How do we know if a command worked or not?

The answer is *exit codes*.

10.3 Exit Codes Tell You If a Command Was Successful

When a command terminates, it tells UNIX what its *exit code* (sometimes called exit *status*) was. You can examine this value by looking at $? after you run a command.

```
> grep gem Gemfile > /dev/null 2>&1
> echo $?
0
> grep gem blah > /dev/null 2>&1
> echo $?
2
```

The exit code is a programmatic way to understand if a command failed without having to parse its output. Although it's up to the command itself to determine what constitutes success, Bash relies strongly on the exit code.

Earlier, we installed NodeJS using `&&` to join three commands together:

```
curl -fsSL https://deb.nodesource.com/setup_22.x -o node_setup.sh && \
    bash node_setup.sh && \
    apt-get install --quiet --yes nodejs"
```

That `&&` means that if the command `curl` exits 0, `bash` should be run and, if it also exits 0, `apt-get install --quiet --yes nodejs` should be run. If `curl` does *not* exit zero, the entire thing will stop and neither `bash` nor `apt-get` will run. It's basically a way to chain commands together stopping when something goes wrong, as shown in "Conditional Execution Based on Exit Codes" on page 67.

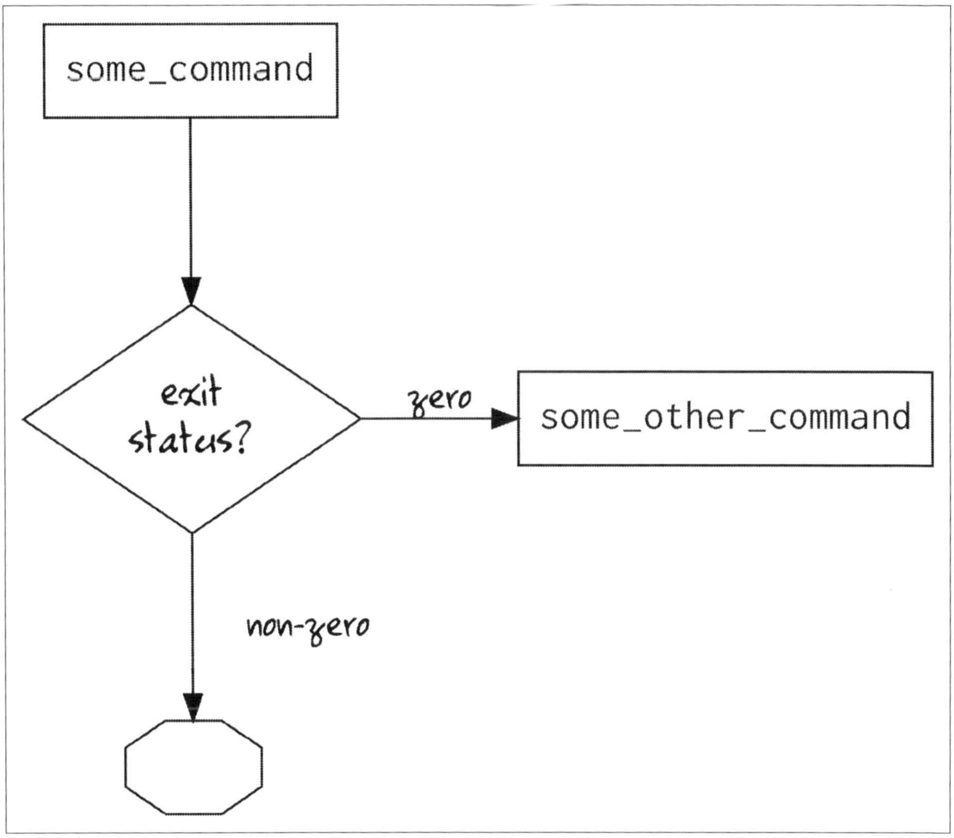

Figure 10.3: Conditional Execution Based on Exit Codes

One caveat if you were tempted to use the `|` operator to combine `curl` and `bash`:

```
curl -fsSL https://deb.nodesource.com/setup_22.x | bash -
```

Bash's default behavior is to ignore the exit code of the first command in a pipeline and to always send its output into the next command in the pipeline. Meaning if `curl` fails, it'll still run `bash`. This is almost never what you want.

To change this, you can run `set -o pipefail` before you run any commands. `set` is a command built-in to Bash that changes its behavior. It will maintain in effect until you exit Bash.

The last thing to know about is how the command line itself is parsed.

10.4 Globbing and Expansion and Escaping

When you do something like `git add *.md`, the `*` in `*.md` is something the shell expands into all the files that end in `.md`. This is called *globbing*. Further, the shell uses spaces to delimit arguments. When you run `grep gem Gemfile`, Bash splits this up by spaces to give three elements: `grep`, assumed to be the command, and then two arguments, `gem`, and `Gemfile`.

10.4.1 Spaces Delimit Arguments, Unless They Are Escaped

If an argument has to have a space in it, you must *escape* it, so that Bash doesn't treat it as an argument delimiter. Suppose our `Gemfile` was called `Gem File`. To perform our grep, we'd need to escape it with a backslash (this is how the multi-line stuff works—the carriage return is escaped):

```
> grep gem Gem\ File
```

Another way to escape it is with double quotes:

```
> grep gem "Gem File"
```

You can use single quotes, too:

```
> grep gem 'Gem File'
```

Single quotes and double quotes have different behavior, however. This difference has to do with *variable expansion*.

10.4.2 Variables Are Expanded... Sometimes

To set a variable in Bash, use = and *no spaces*:

```
SOME_VAR=value
```

Variables don't have to be all caps, but they often are by convention. To refer to this variable you can precede its name with a dollar sign, or surround it with curly braces and use a dollar sign. The latter is generally preferred:

```
> echo ${SOME_VAR}
value
```

Suppose `GEMFILE_NAME` is set to the value of our gem file. The behavior of Bash when using quotes or not is quite different, as is its behavior depending on the type of quote.

`grep gem ${GEMFILE_NAME}` This replaces the variable with its value. If that value has no spaces in it, everything works. If there *are* spaces in it, those spaces are assumed to delimit multiple arguments. This may not be what you want.

`grep gem '${GEMFILE_NAME}'` With single quotes, the variable is not expanded and the literal value `${GEMFILE_NAME}` is used. This is useful when you need to use a literal value that contains special characters like dollar signs and braces.

`grep gem "${GEMFILE_NAME}"` When using double quotes the variable is expanded into its value and the double quotes remain, thus quoting the value. This prevents interpreting spaces as argument delimiters. *This is usually what you want to do in a Bash script.*

I promise you will get used to this nonsense as you write more Bash. Even if you fail to memorize all this behavior, you will at least remember that Bash is a lot fussier than other programming languages.

Let's put this to use and write a script!

11

Writing One Nice Script

> *I was once tasked with building a command line app to run a web server for the team. I collected feedback, sketched prototypes, and arrived at a highly flexible design based on various command line flags. Steve [Jobs] came into the conference room on demo day. Before I could present anything, he picked up a piece of chalk and walked over to the blackboard. He drew a rectangle, then the right-facing angle bracket that represented a UNIX prompt. Next to it, he wrote the word "serve" and said "this is how the app will work" and left the room. I was gobsmacked.*
>
> —*Robert McCool, recounting his time at NeXT*

Let's start with `dx/build`. At its core, it is automating the execution of this command:

```
docker build --file Dockerfile.dev --tag catsay-dev:debian-12.1 .
```

We could throw that into `dx/build` and call it a day, but it would not be as robust as we'd like. In particular:

- What if the script is not run from the root directory? The relative file paths won't work.
- What if Docker isn't installed?
- What if we need to debug the script?
- What if we don't know what `dx/build` does and are afraid to run it?

Let's tackle each one of these.

11.1 Turning Relative Paths Into Absolute Paths

Suppose we are working out of `/home/chris/projects/personal/catsay`, meaning we'll expect our script to be in `/home/chris/projects/personal/catsay/dx/build`. What we want to do is run this command:

```
docker build  \
  --file /home/chris/projects/personal/catsay/Dockerfile.dev  \
  --tag catsay-dev:debian-12.1 \
  /home/chris/projects/personal/catsay/
```

We know that the project root directory is the parent directory of where the script is. What you may not know is that `${0}` is set in all Bash scripts to be the path to the current script. Further, `pwd` is a command to get the full path of wherever our current working directory is, and `dirname` prints out the path to a file, without the file's name.

This is all we need to determine the project's root directory. What we'll do is get the `dirname` of our script (`${0}`), `cd` there and capture the value of `pwd`. This is our `SCRIPT_DIR`. We'll then `cd` to the `..` of `SCRIPT_DIR` and capture `pwd` there. That's our `ROOT_DIR`.

To capture the output of a command into a variable, you can use `VAR=$(command)`, like so:

```
DIRNAME=$(dirname "${0}") # => dx
SCRIPT_DIR=$(cd "${DIRNAME}" && pwd)
```

This isn't completely robust, however. Since these invocations are ultimately assembling strings from the command line, there are some issues that can arise. What if `DIRNAME` has a dash in it? That could be interpreted as a command line flag. What if `cd` outputs something? Then, `SCRIPT_DIR` would have that output in its value. We don't want that.

Most UNIX commands recognize `--` to mean "this is the end of flags that start with a -". We already know how to direct output to `/dev/null`, so this means what we want is:

```
DIRNAME=$(dirname -- "${0}") # => dx
SCRIPT_DIR=$(cd -- "${DIRNAME}" > /dev/null 2>&1 && pwd)
ROOT_DIR=$(cd -- "${SCRIPT_DIR}/".. > /dev/null 2>&1 && pwd)
```

Let's try it! We'll create `dx/build`. The first line of the script has to be the so-called *shebang* that indicates this is a Bash script. The first line of a script in a UNIX system tells UNIX what program to use to interpret the script. It must be a full path. Usually Bash is available at `/bin/bash`, but this is not always the case. It is more likely the case that `/usr/bin/env` exists, and `env` will locate a command to run, as long as that command is in the path.

Thus, our script can start with `#!/usr/bin/env bash`, which tells UNIX to tell `env` to find `bash` in our path and use that. This should keep the script as portable as possible across operating systems.

We'll also want to set that "pipefail" setting we saw back in Exit Codes Tell You If a Command Was Successful on page 66. *And* we want to use another setting that tells Bash to stop running if any command exits nonzero, which is `set -e`.

For now, we'll just `echo` the values of the variables to see that they are correct.

```
# dx/build

#!/usr/bin/env bash

set -e
set -o pipefail

DIRNAME=$(dirname -- "${0}")
SCRIPT_DIR=$(cd -- "${DIRNAME}" > /dev/null 2>&1 && pwd)
ROOT_DIR=$(cd -- "${SCRIPT_DIR}"/.. > /dev/null 2>&1 && pwd)
echo $SCRIPT_DIR ; echo $ROOT_DIR
```

We'll need to make it executable via `chmod +x`:

```
> chmod +x dx/build
```

And now, it should run and show us both the full path to where the script is and the full path to where the project root is. Keep in mind you will see a different value than me, since we likely aren't working out of the same directory:

```
> dx/build
/root/work/catsay/dx
/root/work/catsay
```

Great! Now let's check to see if Docker is installed.

11.2 Checking Nicely if Command Line Utilities Exist

If someone runs `dx/build` without having installed Docker, by default they will get an unhelpful message like:

```
> bin/dx
bash: docker: command not found
```

This is not a good experience, especially if it's your first time running the script. It's not clear where that message came from or what to do about it. To make a better experience, we want to check to see if `docker` is installed and, if not, produce a more useful message before exiting the script.

To do this, Bash includes a *builtin* called `command`. Bash builtins aren't command line utilities like `ls` or `grep`. They are more like a keyword built into a programming language, thus "builtin". To get help on builtins, use `help`:

```
> help command
command: command [-pVv] command [arg ...]
    Runs COMMAND with ARGS ignoring shell functions.
    If you have a shell function called `ls', and you
    wish to call the command `ls', you can say
    "command ls".  If the -p option is given, a
    default value is used for PATH that is guaranteed
    to find all of the standard utilities.  If the -V
    or -v option is given, a string is printed
    describing COMMAND. The -V option produces a more
    verbose description.
```

There's a lot going on here, but the part we can use is `-v`, which will not execute the command but print out a string of where it is. More crucially, `command` will exit 0 if it finds the command and nonzero if it doesn't. This means we can use the exit code as part of an `if` statement.

Because we don't want the user to see the output of `command`, we'll redirect its standard output and standard error to `/dev/null`. The entire invocation will be `command -v "docker" > /dev/null 2>&1`. We can put that directly into an `if` statement.

Here's what it looks like, with `docker` purposefully misspelled so we can test the logic.

```
# dx/build

  DIRNAME=$(dirname -- "${0}")
  SCRIPT_DIR=$(cd -- "${DIRNAME}" > /dev/null 2>&1 && pwd)
  ROOT_DIR=$(cd -- "${SCRIPT_DIR}"/.. > /dev/null 2>&1 && pwd)
→ if ! command -v "dcker" > /dev/null 2>&1; then
→   echo "Docker is not installed."
→   echo "Please visit https://docs.docker.com/get-docker/"
→   exit 1
→ fi
```

Note that we explicitly exit nonzero in this case, because the script was not able to do what was requested of it.

If this is your first time seeing an `if` statement in Bash, a few things to note:

- The spaces between things are important and if you omit them, it may not work right. This is somewhat different from other programming languages.
- You end the `if` with the word `if` spelled backwards, which is `fi`. I wish I was making that up, but wait until we use a `case` statement.

Let's run it. We'll use `||` to echo a message if the prior command exited nonzero. This is like the opposite of `&&` and is an easy way to check that our script did not exit with a 0.

```
> dx/build || echo command exited nonzero
Docker is not installed.
Please visit https://docs.docker.com/get-docker/
command exited nonzero
```

That shows our logic is good, so let's change `dcker` to `docker`:

```
# dx/build

  DIRNAME=$(dirname -- "${0}")
  SCRIPT_DIR=$(cd -- "${DIRNAME}" > /dev/null 2>&1 && pwd)
  ROOT_DIR=$(cd -- "${SCRIPT_DIR}"/.. > /dev/null 2>&1 && pwd)
→ if ! command -v "docker" > /dev/null 2>&1; then
    echo "Docker is not installed."
    echo "Please visit https://docs.docker.com/get-docker/"
    exit 1
```

Debugging Bash scripts is notoriously difficult, and these scripts in particular can benefit from more verbosity, since they are being run in degenerate environments where errors are more likely.

11.3 Understanding What the Script is Doing

Observability is the buzzword for understanding what your code is actually doing. For command line scripts, the only real way to achieve this is with `echo` statements. There are three approaches people take for observability of command line scripts:

- Print only errors, the so-called "No news is good news" philosophy.
- Print out everything that's happening no matter what.
- Print out everything that's happening if a `--verbose` flag is given, or if a `--quiet` flag is omitted.

The third option is the best in a general sense, but for our purposes, always showing what's happening will be better. It'll help us when writing the scripts and also make sure that any error a future user experiences will be easy to diagnose without having to know about re-running it with `--verbose`.

The approach to take will be as follows:

- Before any action, print out the action that's going to be taken, in human language, including any derived values.

- Make sure that every possible outcome of the action generates another printed message, again in human language.
- Ensure that every message is clearly marked as coming from the script, to distinguish these messages from any other output that gets generated.

This approach means that a user of the script will always know what the script was doing and what happened, even in the event of an error. They will also be able to see which messages were from the script and which weren't.

Rather than use `echo`, let's create a function that prefixes all messages with the script's name. To make a function in Bash, you write the function's name, followed by parens, followed by a brace, followed by the code, followed by another brace:

```
log() {
  # code goes here
}
```

Bash functions don't take named arguments. If you want the first argument passed to a function, you use `${1}`. If you want the forty-second, you use `${42}`. You can also use `${@}` to represent *all* passed arguments, properly quoted and suitable for passing through to another command. That's what we'll use to make our `log` function, since it will basically pass all the args to `echo`.

Note that `${0}` still represents the path to the script, even inside a function. We'll use that to construct our prefix.

```
# dx/build

  DIRNAME=$(dirname -- "${0}")
  SCRIPT_DIR=$(cd -- "${DIRNAME}" > /dev/null 2>&1 && pwd)
  ROOT_DIR=$(cd -- "${SCRIPT_DIR}"/.. > /dev/null 2>&1 && pwd)
→ log() {
→   echo "[ ${0} ]" "${@}"
→ } # log
→
  if ! command -v "docker" > /dev/null 2>&1; then
    echo "Docker is not installed."
    echo "Please visit https://docs.docker.com/get-docker/"
```

Right now, we have two `echo` statements inside our `if` that checks for the existence of Docker. Let's replace those with calls to `log`:

```
# dx/build

    echo "[ ${0} ]" "${@}"
  } # log

  if ! command -v "docker" > /dev/null 2>&1; then
× #  echo "Docker is not installed."
× #  echo "Please visit https://docs.docker.com/get-docker/"
→   log "Docker is not installed."
→   log "Please visit https://docs.docker.com/get-docker/"
    exit 1
  fi
```

Next, let's add a `log` call after the check, to affirm that we found Docker:

```
# dx/build

    log "Please visit https://docs.docker.com/get-docker/"
    exit 1
  fi
→ log "Docker is installed!"
```

No matter what happens when the script runs, the user is going to see messages that are clearly from the script that explain what the script did or what's happening.

```
> dx/build
[ dx/build ] Docker is installed!
```

The last thing to do—other than adding the actual call to `docker build`—is provide a way for a user to get help.

11.4 Allow The User to Ask for Help

It's traditional on UNIX command line utilities to respond to `-h` with some documentation. A user may expect to be able to run `dx/build -h` and get some information on what the script does and what options there are. The user will also expect that the script will not do anything in this case, thus making it always safe to use `-h`.

We could certainly check to see if the first argument to our script was `-h`, but users sometimes do weird things, like run `dx/build foo -h` and expect the `-h` to trigger help. We can handle this situation by using the `getopts` command.

`getopts` is an *incredibly* strange command, but it will do what we want. To use it, we'll give it a string describing the flags that we accept, the name of a variable where a parsed flag will be placed, and `"${@}"`, which we saw earlier and is a special variable that, when quoted, provides access to all the command line arguments.

Each time you call `getopts`, it exits 0 if it parsed a single flag and exits nonzero if there aren't any more flags to parse. Thus, it must be called repeatedly in a loop.

The string that specifies the flags to accept is very strange, so prepare yourself.

- It must start with a colon, or `getopts` will output errors to the user that don't make sense and that we cannot control.
- After that colon, each letter in the string represents a command line flag to recognize, so e.g. `h` would mean we accept `-h`.
- After each letter, an optional colon can appear that indicates that flag requires an argument, so e.g. `f:` would allow for something like `-f Dockerfile`.
- If the optional colon is omitted, that flag must not receive an argument, so e.g. `i` would mean that `-i foo` would be considered an error.

OK, so this is weird and strange, but we're not done yet.

Given that want to only accept `-h`, the string we want is `":h"`, making the invocation to `getopts` look like so:

```
getopts ":h" opt "${@}"
```

We want to call it in a loop until it exits non-zero:

```
while getopts ":h" opt "${@}"; do
  # ${opt} has a value here
end
```

What happens inside our loop is weird and complicated, as outlined in "Parsing Command Line Flags" on page 79.

Each time we call `getopts`:

- If it is done parsing, it exits nonzero and the loop exits.
- If a valid argument is parsed, that letter is placed into `${opt}`.
- In an invalid argument is parsed, `${opt}` will have the value `?` and the invalid letter is placed in `${OPTARG}`. This is how we can create a useful error message.

While we could implement this logic using an `if` statement, it's more conventional to use `case` because it is easier to adapt when additional arguments are needed.

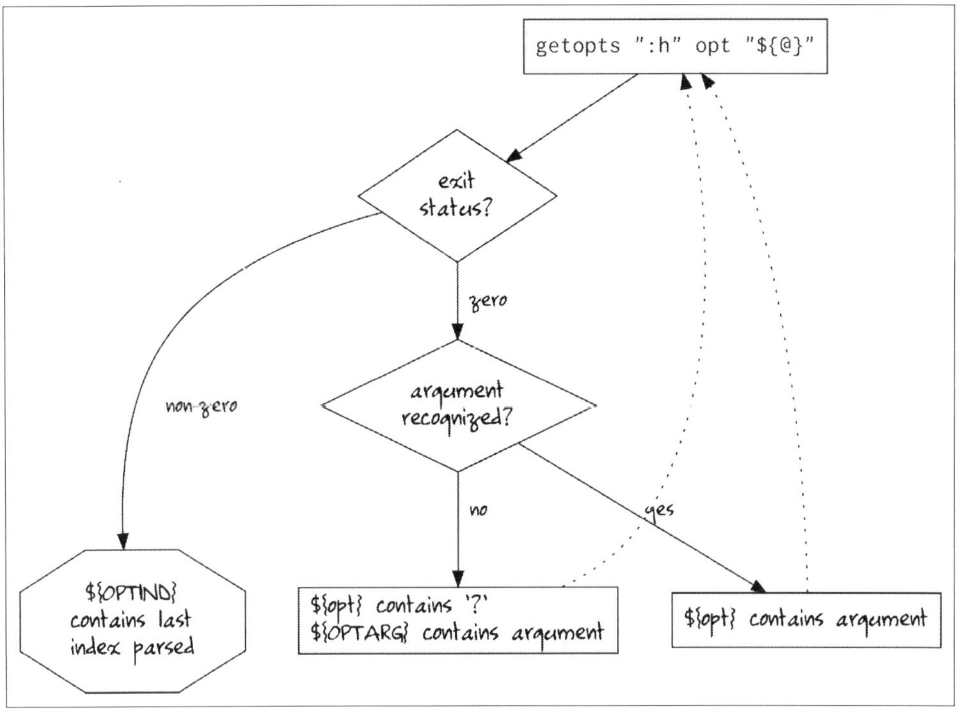

Figure 11.1: Parsing Command Line Flags

It will also look familiar to anyone who has already done this, making the script more approachable.

Here's how it will look. When we get the `-h` we'll call a to-be-defined function named `usage`, then exit 0 (since the script did what was asked of it). If we get any other flag, we'll output an error, then call `usage`, then exit nonzero.

```
# dx/build

  log() {
    echo "[ ${0} ]" "${@}"
  } # log
→
→ while getopts ":h" opt "${@}"; do
→   case ${opt} in
→     h)
→       usage
→       exit 0
→       ;;
→     ?)
→       log "Invalid option: ${OPTARG}"
→       usage
```

```
→         exit 1
→         ;;
→     esac
→ done
→

  if ! command -v "docker" > /dev/null 2>&1; then
    log "Docker is not installed."
```

Yes, case statements end with the word "case" spelled backwards: esac. I'm not sure if I should be surprised or relieved that while doesn't end in elihw.

One other convention is to remove all the parsed flags from ${@}. That makes it easier if the script wants to do something with non-flag arguments. As shown in the diagram, getopts sets the variable OPTIND as the index into the argument list where it left off. We can use shift to remove that many arguments from ${@}:

```
# dx/build

        ;;
    esac
  done
→ shift $((OPTIND -1))


  if ! command -v "docker" > /dev/null 2>&1; then
```

Now, if we need to look at the unparsed arguments, ${@} contains them, but not the command line flags getopts recognized.

I want to stress that figuring this out is not easy. You should not expect yourself to have cruised through the documentation and arrived at this odd construct. The way *I* figured it out was to find a working example on Stack Overflow, then went into the docs to understand what each part did.

We still need to define usage. We'll put the code for it after the code for log. Note that we aren't using log to output information from usage. This is somewhat subjective, but makes sense in this context, since the prefix of the command name will gunk up the help output. The user knows that the output they are seeing is from the use of -h.

```
# dx/build

  log() {
    echo "[ ${0} ]" "${@}"
```

```
  } # log
→
→ usage() {
→   echo "usage: $0 [-h]"
→   echo ""
→   echo "Builds the development Docker image from Dockerfile.dev"
→   echo ""
→   echo "OPTIONS"
→   echo ""
→   echo "  -h - show this help"
→ } # usage

  while getopts ":h" opt "${@}"; do
    case ${opt} in
```

Let's try it:

```
> dx/build -h
usage: dx/build [-h]

Builds the development Docker image from Dockerfile.dev

OPTIONS

  -h - show this help

> dx/build -q || echo command exited nonzero
[ dx/build ] Invalid option: q
usage: dx/build [-h]

Builds the development Docker image from Dockerfile.dev

OPTIONS

  -h - show this help
command exited nonzero
```

Nice! And *now* we can add our single line of code to call `docker build`.

11.5 Adding What We Want to Automate

Before we add our command, we need to think about the aspects of our script that we just spent time setting up, namely that the script will output what it's doing. To that end, the script should output that it's going to build a Docker image and include the image name in that message. Thus, we want the image name in a variable.

Here's how all that looks (remember that to assign a variable, you *must not* have spaces around the =).

```
# dx/build

    exit 1
  fi
  log "Docker is installed!"
→ IMAGE=catsay-dev:debian-12.1
→
→ log "Building Docker image '${IMAGE}'"
→ docker build \
→   --quiet \
→   --file "${ROOT_DIR}/Dockerfile.dev" \
→   --tag "${IMAGE}" \
→   "${ROOT_DIR}"
→
→ log "Docker image '${IMAGE}'" is built
```

Note the use of single quotes around the image name in the calls to `log`. This makes sure *something* shows up. If, for whatever reason, `IMAGE` doesn't get set, instead of seeing "Docker image is built", you'd see "Docker image ' ' is built" which would look odd, cueing you that there may be a problem. And, of course, because those single quotes are inside double quotes, the variable `${IMAGE}` is expanded and will appear in the message to the user.

You don't have to call `exit 0` because that is the default behavior when execution reaches the end of the script. This means, we're done and can build the image:

```
> dx/build
[ dx/build ] Docker is installed!
[ dx/build ] Building Docker image 'catsay-dev:debian-12.1'
sha256:7c7032317d90b36adc853fb651dc33328fb471b83bb34a537d229. . .
[ dx/build ] Docker image 'catsay-dev:debian-12.1' is built
```

Notice how, in the output, three lines are prefixed with `[ dx/build ]` and one is not. This is a strong clue to the user that the oddball line is coming from somewhere else. And, because we are logging everything that happens, it's likely that the message is coming from `docker build`.

Now, let's draw the rest of the owl.

12

Build the Remaining Scripts

Last thing, still, no one is owning up to the nonzero exit code. I wanna clarify that it's not so much the nonzero exit code, but rather the fact that no one is taking responsibility for the nonzero exit code. We're not first year CS students. It's okay to make mistakes. We can accidentally exit nonzero, but we need to own up to it with immediacy, integrity, and honesty. Does anyone wanna talk any more about the nonzero exit code?

—Curtis Duffy, Michelin-starred Chef and UNIX Hacker

With what we learned in the last chapter, we should have no problems creating `dx/start`, `dx/stop`, and `dx/exec`. But, that would be a bunch of copy and paste. We'd like to apply at least *some* good practices for software engineering to this. We can. . . to an extent. Let's go ahead and write `dx/start` via copy and paste, and then see how we can reduce the duplication that creates.

12.1 Automating Dev Env Startup

`dx/start` will automate the execution of `docker compose --file docker-compose.dev.yml up --detach`. In many ways, this script is almost exactly like `dx/build`, and this will be a great way to understand code re-use in Bash.

Here is the entire script that meets the same criteria as `dx/build`, including a ton of duplicated code that we saw in the last chapter:

```
# dx/start

#!/bin/bash

set -e
set -o pipefail

DIRNAME=$(dirname -- "${0}")
SCRIPT_DIR=$(cd -- "${DIRNAME}" > /dev/null 2>&1 && pwd)
ROOT_DIR=$(cd -- "${SCRIPT_DIR}"/.. > /dev/null 2>&1 && pwd)
log() {
```

```
  echo "[ ${0} ]" "${@}"
} # log

usage() {
  echo "usage: $0 [-h]"
  echo ""
  echo "Starts the development environment"
  echo ""
  echo "OPTIONS"
  echo ""
  echo "  -h - show this help"
} # usage

while getopts ":h" opt "${@}"; do
  case ${opt} in
    h)
      usage
      exit 0
      ;;
    ?)
      log "Invalid option: ${OPTARG}"
      usage
      exit 1
      ;;
  esac
done
shift $((OPTIND -1))


if ! command -v "docker" > /dev/null 2>&1; then
  log "Docker is not installed."
  log "Please visit https://docs.docker.com/get-docker/"
  exit 1
fi
log "Docker is installed!"

log "Starting dev environment"
docker compose \
  --ansi=never \
  --file "${ROOT_DIR}"/docker-compose.dev.yml \
  up \
    --detach \
    --no-color

log "Dev environment started"
```

As programmers, we tend to take a dim view of so much copy and paste. Ideally, things that are the same can be extracted to a central place and re-used. Here are a few things jump out as being duplicative:

- The determination of `SCRIPT_DIR` and `ROOT_DIR`
- The `log` function
- The use of `getopts`
- Checking for `docker`'s existence

The main way to extract and share code in Bash is to create a new file and *source* it, which is done using a single `.`, like so:

```
. shared.lib.sh
```

This will behave as if the entirety of `shared.lib.sh` had been pasted right where that line of code is.

The problem, however is that you must safely locate that file to source it, and doing that requires the `SCRIPT_DIR`. Meaning: we can't extract code to determine `SCRIPT_DIR` and re-use it across all scripts. It'll have to be duplicated in each script.

Another issue is that even though `dx/build` and `dx/start` currently accept the same command line arguments, `dx/exec` won't (as we'll see later). Extracting the use of `getopts` into a function presupposes that all of our scripts will accept the same command line arguments. This isn't going to be true. Thus, we'll need to keep that duplication, too.

But, `log` and the `docker` check can be shared, as well as the determination of `ROOT_DIR` (so long as `SCRIPT_DIR` is defined before we source the shared code. We'll put this shared code in `dx/shared.lib.sh`. Since it will require `SCRIPT_DIR` to be defined, we'll need to check for that in case someone uses the file without defining it (in Bash, undefined variables expand to the empty string, so we can't expect a failure to happen if the variable has no value).

12.1.1 Bash Conditionals Are Odd

To check if a variable is defined, it's common to check if the variable expands to the empty string. Previously, we saw that `if` takes a command that is executed. If that command exits zero, the `if` condition is considered true. Way back in the early days of Unix, there was a command named `[` (open square bracket). That command accepted various command line arguments and required that the very last argument be a literal `]` (closing square bracket). `[` is now a built-in (like `command`).

`[` accepts the flag `-z` which itself requires an argument. `[ -z «some value»` exits zero if `«some value»` is empty. This is not only exactly what we need, but a helluva way to implement conditional logic. Here's what it looks like:

```
if [ -z $SCRIPT_DIR ]; then
  log "SCRIPT_DIR was not defined"
  exit 1
fi
```

For the longest time, I thought `[` and `]` were like parenthesis in other languages. But, as we just found out, `[` is a command, and it merely requires `]` to give the appearance of an expression. It also explains why you have to have a space after `[` and before `]`. If you wrote `if [-z $SCRIPT_DIR]`, Bash would try to run the command named `[-z]` with the argument `$SCRIPT_DIR]`. Bash is wild.

You'll notice that we used `log` to produce an error message. This means we have to define `log` before we do the check. Not a problem.

```
# dx/shared.lib.sh

log() {
  echo "[ ${0} ]" "${@}"
} # log

if [ -z $SCRIPT_DIR ]; then
  log "SCRIPT_DIR was not defined"
  exit 1
fi

ROOT_DIR=$(cd -- "${SCRIPT_DIR}"/.. > /dev/null 2>&1 && pwd)
```

Since this file is going to be sourced, we should not put the shebang at the top or call `set -e`. That provides a clue that this is a re-usable file and reduces the chance it will do something if someone runs it (we also won't be marking it as executable).

12.1.2 Creating Re-usable Functions

For the Docker check, we could copy the `if` statement, however it may create a somewhat awkward experience. Suppose Docker was not installed, but the user had executed `dx/start -h`. Instead of showing help, the script would exit because Docker's not installed. Suppose Docker *is* installed, and the user mistakenly executed `dx/start -q`. This would print a message saying that Docker was installed, and then show an error message.

We don't want this. To get around it, we'll define a function named `check_for_docker` that executes the `if` statement. Each script would call that when the time was right.

```
# dx/shared.lib.sh

    log "SCRIPT_DIR was not defined"
    exit 1
  fi
→
→ check_for_docker() {
→   if ! command -v "docker" > /dev/null 2>&1; then
→     log "Docker is not installed."
→     log "Please visit https://docs.docker.com/get-docker/"
→     exit 1
→   fi
→   log "Docker is installed!"
→ }
→

  ROOT_DIR=$(cd -- "${SCRIPT_DIR}"/.. > /dev/null 2>&1 && pwd)
```

Remember, since sourcing `dx/shared.lib.sh` is the same as pasting the entire file into our script, any function (or variable) we define is available. Bash has no concept of private members or information hiding.

12.1.3 Using Shared Code

Now that we have some re-usable code in `dx/shared.lib.sh`, we can refactor `dx/start` to use it. First, we'll source the file right after we determine `SCRIPT_DIR`:

```
# dx/start

  set -o pipefail

  DIRNAME=$(dirname -- "${0}")
  SCRIPT_DIR=$(cd -- "${DIRNAME}" > /dev/null 2>&1 && pwd)
× #ROOT_DIR=$(cd -- "${SCRIPT_DIR}"/.. > /dev/null 2>&1 && pwd)
× #log() {
× #  echo "[ ${0} ]" "${@}"
× #} # log
→ . "${SCRIPT_DIR}"/shared.lib.sh

  usage() {
    echo "usage: $0 [-h]"
```

Next, we can remove the `docker` check in favor of calling `check_for_docker`:

```
# dx/start

  done
  shift $((OPTIND -1))


× #if ! command -v "docker" > /dev/null 2>&1; then
× #  log "Docker is not installed."
× #  log "Please visit https://docs.docker.com/get-docker/"
× #  exit 1
× #fi
× #log "Docker is installed!"
→ check_for_docker

  log "Starting dev environment"
  docker compose \
```

We can use dx/shared.lib.sh to create dx/build but before we do that, there's one thing we'll need to manage wasn't relevant to dx/start's code, which is the name of the Docker image. It's needed in dx/build *and* in docker-compose.dev.yml. We'll want everything to use the same definition of the name.

12.2 Putting Shared Values in an .env File

Docker Compose has the ability to substitute environment variables[1]. That means that we could do something like this:

```
services:
  app:
    image: ${IMAGE}
    volumes:
      # ...
```

As long as IMAGE was set in the UNIX environment when we call docker compose, it will work and use IMAGE's value. If you aren't familiar, the UNIX environment is a set of keys and values available to any process. You can examine your UNIX environment right now by running env (which is the same /usr/bin/env we used in our shebang to locate Bash).

In order to allow dx/build and docker-compose.dev.yml to share the value for the image name, we'll need a single place where it's stored that they both can access. One option is to have dx/start *export* the value when it runs docker compose.

[1] https://docs.docker.com/compose/environment-variables/set-environment-variables

When a Bash script runs another command, that command will inherit the Bash script's UNIX environment. *However*, setting a variable in a Bash script does not place that variable into the UNIX environment. To arrange that, we'd need to use `export`, like so:

```
IMAGE=«some value»
export IMAGE
docker compose \
  # ...
```

While it's nice that this works, I find this sort of convoluted implicit behavior confusing and difficult to observe. It beats duplication, but Docker provides a better way to share information. `docker compose` supports a flag called `--env-var` that accepts a file contain environment variables. The format of this file is the same as the format for declaring variables in Bash!

```
IMAGE=catsay-dev:debian-12.1
```

That means we can put this declaration into a file, source it in our Bash scripts, and use it with `--env-var` when calling `docker compose`. No need to manage UNIX environments or `export`.

We don't want this in `dx/shared.lib.sh` for two reasons. First, `dx/shared.lib.sh` can't be used as a Docker Compose environment variables file. Second, the image name it will contain is specific to this project, whereas everything else we've done inside `dx/` is project-agnostic. It'll be better to keep them in separate files. But, to avoid another location, we'll put the file in `dx/` since it's related to the dev environment. We'll call the file `dx/docker-compose.env`.

```
# dx/docker-compose.env

# The name of the image built by dx/build
IMAGE=catsay-dev:debian-12.1
```

Now, we can change `docker-compose.dev.yml` to reference this new variable:

```
# docker-compose.dev.yml

  services:
```

```
    app:
→     image: ${IMAGE}
      init: true
      volumes:
        - type: bind
```

And we'll add --env-file to our invocation of docker compose in dx/start:

```
# dx/start


  check_for_docker

  log "Starting dev environment"
× #docker compose \
× #   --ansi=never \
× #   --file "${ROOT_DIR}"/docker-compose.dev.yml \
× #   up \
× #     --detach \
× #     --no-color
→ docker compose \
→   --ansi=never \
→   --env-file "${SCRIPT_DIR}"/docker-compose.env \
→   --file "${ROOT_DIR}"/docker-compose.dev.yml \
→   up \
→     --detach \
→     --no-color

  log "Dev environment started"
```

Now, back to dx/build. It will look very similar to dx/start, but with as much of the duplication removed as possible. Here's the entire script:

```
# dx/build

#!/bin/bash

set -e
set -o pipefail

DIRNAME=$(dirname -- "${0}")
SCRIPT_DIR=$(cd -- "${DIRNAME}" > /dev/null 2>&1 && pwd)
```

```
. "${SCRIPT_DIR}"/shared.lib.sh
. "${SCRIPT_DIR}"/docker-compose.env

usage() {
  echo "usage: $0 [-h]"
  echo ""
  echo "Builds the development Docker image from Dockerfile.dev"
  echo ""
  echo "OPTIONS"
  echo ""
  echo "  -h - show this help"
} # usage

while getopts ":h" opt "${@}"; do
  case ${opt} in
    h)
      usage
      exit 0
      ;;
    ?)
      log "Invalid option: ${OPTARG}"
      usage
      exit 1
      ;;
  esac
done
shift $((OPTIND -1))

check_for_docker

log "Building Docker image '${IMAGE}'"
docker build \
  --quiet \
  --file "${ROOT_DIR}"/Dockerfile.dev \
  --tag "${IMAGE}" \
  "${ROOT_DIR}"

log "Docker image '${IMAGE}'" is built
```

12.3 Automating Shutdown

dx/stop will look very similar to dx/start, except it will call docker compose stop. Here's what it should look like, remembering that we've done our best to eliminate what duplication we can:

```
# dx/stop

#!/bin/bash

set -e
set -o pipefail

DIRNAME=$(dirname -- "${0}")
SCRIPT_DIR=$(cd -- "${DIRNAME}" > /dev/null 2>&1 && pwd)
. "${SCRIPT_DIR}"/shared.lib.sh

usage() {
  echo "usage: $0 [-h]"
  echo ""
  echo "Stops the development environment"
  echo ""
  echo "OPTIONS"
  echo ""
  echo "  -h - show this help"
} # usage

while getopts ":h" opt "${@}"; do
  case ${opt} in
    h)
      usage
      exit 0
      ;;
    ?)
      log "Invalid option: ${OPTARG}"
      usage
      exit 1
      ;;
  esac
done
shift $((OPTIND -1))

check_for_docker

log "Stopping dev environment"
docker compose \
  --env-file "${SCRIPT_DIR}"/docker-compose.env \
  --ansi=never \
  --file "${ROOT_DIR}"/docker-compose.dev.yml \
  down

log "Dev environment stopped"
```

I know this duplication doesn't feel good. But, the duplicated code is relatively stable. It's unlikely to have to change, and thus we're unlikely to have to make the same change more than once.

We're almost ready to use these scripts. We just need to write `dx/exec`.

12.4 Automating Execution Inside a Container

`dx/exec` will need to do two things that our other scripts don't. First, it needs to accept the command line to run inside the container. Second, it should accept a command-line flag to indicate the name of the container where the command should be run.

While you are almost always going to run commands inside `app` (the name of the service in `docker-compose.dev.yml` where we configure our app), you may want to run commands inside other containers. For example, you might want to run `redis-cli` inside the Redis container to poke around at Redis directly.

Let's start it off like the others, but let's set a new variable named `SERVICE` that will store the default value: `app`. This will be used in our `docker container exec` command and be overridable by `-s`:

```
# dx/exec

#!/bin/bash

set -e
set -o pipefail

DIRNAME=$(dirname -- "${0}")
SCRIPT_DIR=$(cd -- "${DIRNAME}" > /dev/null 2>&1 && pwd)
. "${SCRIPT_DIR}"/shared.lib.sh

# Default service commands are exec'ed in
SERVICE=app
```

Next, we'll need to implement `usage`, which will outline the `-s` flag as well as what the arguments to the command mean. Because this creates a few different ways to invoke it, we'll add some examples to the output. Note that we are using the `SERVICE` variable in the output so it stays consistent with whatever the default is.

```
# dx/exec


  # Default service commands are exec'ed in
  SERVICE=app
→
```

```
→ usage() {
→   echo "usage: $0 [-h] [-s service] command"
→   echo ""
→   echo "Executes a command inside a container"
→   echo ""
→   echo "OPTIONS"
→   echo ""
→   echo "  -s service - Set the service name for the"
→   echo "               command (defaults to '${SERVICE}')"
→   echo "  -h         - show this help"
→   echo ""
→   echo "ARGUMENTS"
→   echo ""
→   echo "  command - a command line to execute inside the container"
→   echo ""
→   echo "EXAMPLES"
→   echo ""
→   echo "  # 'log in' to the '${SERVICE}' container"
→   echo "  dx/exec bash"
→   echo ""
→   echo "  # run bin/setup in the '${SERVICE}' container"
→   echo "  dx/exec bin/setup"
→   echo ""
→   echo "  # run 'redis-cli' in the 'redis' container"
→   echo "  dx/exec -s redis redis-cli"
→ } # usage
```

Now, we need to make our usage documentation truthful by writing the `getopts` part. Here, the string we'll give is `":hs:"`. The newly-added `s:` indicates that we accept a `-s` and that it requires an argument. When that happens, the argument's value will be placed in `OPTARG`. We'll use that to change the value of `SERVICE`. This arcane way of describing the options is outlined in figure "Decoding `getopts` Strings" on page 94.

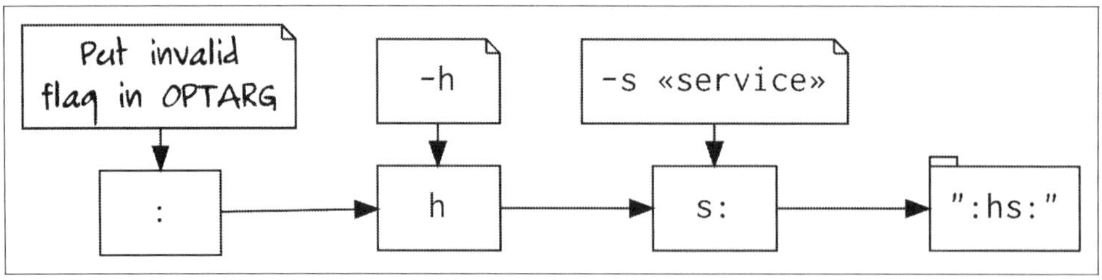

Figure 12.1: Decoding `getopts` Strings

```
# dx/exec
```

```
    echo "  # run 'redis-cli' in the 'redis' container"
    echo "  dx/exec -s redis redis-cli"
  } # usage

  while getopts ":hs:" opt "${@}"; do
    case ${opt} in
      s)
        SERVICE="${OPTARG}"
        ;;
      h)
        usage
        exit 0
        ;;
      ?)
        log "Invalid option: ${OPTARG}"
        usage
        exit 1
        ;;
    esac
  done
  shift $((OPTIND -1))
```

Next, we'll call `check_for_docker` then the invocation of `docker compose exec`. Note that the final argument to `docker compose exec` is `"${@}"`. Because we used `shift` after the loop that called `getopts`, `${@}` now contains only the parts of the command line that were not parsed. These parts are assumed to be the command to execute. See the figure "Command Line Parsing" on page 95.

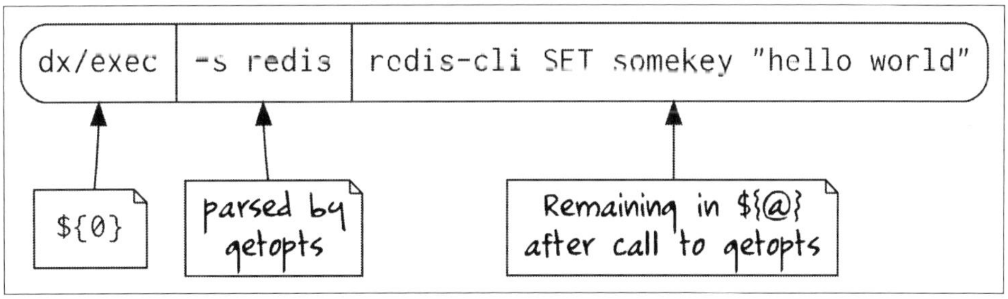

Figure 12.2: Command Line Parsing

Here's the rest of the script:

```
# dx/exec

    esac
  done
  shift $((OPTIND -1))
```

```
→
→ check_for_docker
→
→ log "Executing '${@}' inside container with service named '${SERVICE}'"
→ docker compose \
→   --env-file "${SCRIPT_DIR}"/docker-compose.env \
→   --ansi=never \
→   --file "${ROOT_DIR}"/docker-compose.dev.yml \
→   exec \
→     "${SERVICE}" \
→     "${@}"
→
→ log "Execution complete"
```

We need to make all these scripts executable:

```
> chmod +x dx/start dx/stop dx/build dx/exec
```

And now, we can perform our workflow.

12.5 Executing the Improved Workflow

First, let's build the container:

```
> dx/build
«lots of output»
```

Now, we can start it all up:

```
> dx/start
«lots of output»
```

Now, we can do development. We'll start with `bin/setup`:

```
> dx/exec bin/setup
«lots of output»
```

We should still be able to run the app with `bin/run` and see the app running on `localhost:4242`, as shown in what I promise you is a different screenshot taken from this particular execution on page 97.

```
> dx/exec bin/run
```

When we are done working for the day, everything can be shut down:

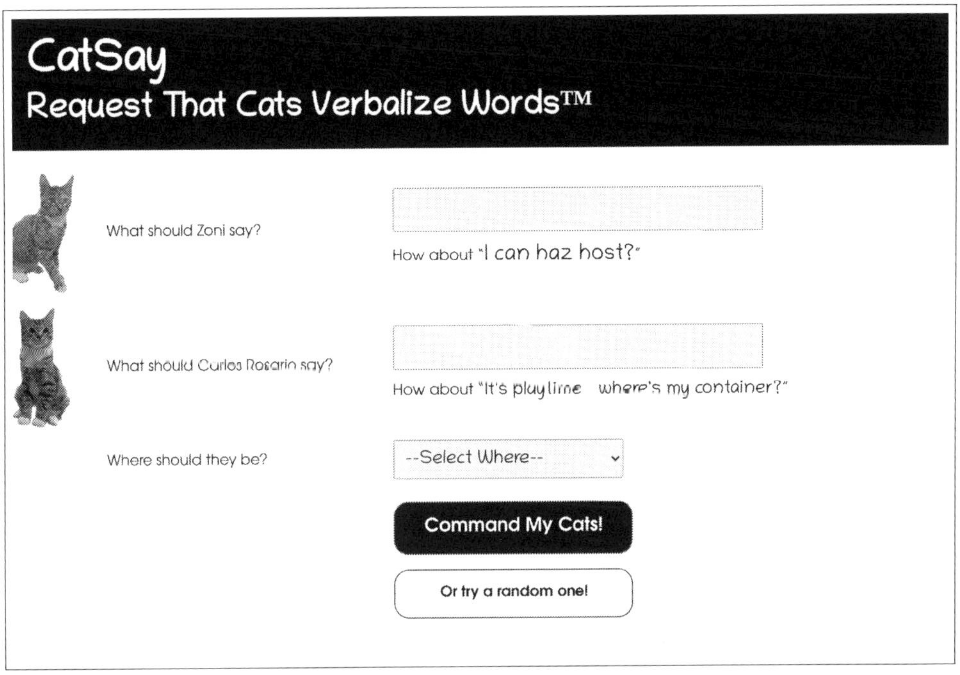

Figure 12.3: CatSay Homepage Again

```
> dx/stop
[ dx/stop ] Docker is installed!
[ dx/stop ] Stopping dev environment
 Container catsay-redis-1  Stopping
 Container catsay-app-1  Stopping
 Container catsay-app-1  Stopped
 Container catsay-app-1  Removing
 Container catsay-redis-1  Stopped
 Container catsay-redis-1  Removing
 Container catsay-redis-1  Removed
 Container catsay-app-1  Removed
 Network catsay_default  Removing
 Network catsay_default  Removed
[ dx/stop ] Dev environment stopped
```

This is a great development workflow. This means that the documentation for setting up a dev environment boils down to:

1. Install Docker
2. Clone the repo/source code for the app
3. `dx/build`
4. `dx/start`
5. `dx/exec «command»`

And this is from a completely new computer. A new team member can be up and running their dev environment in *minutes, especially* if you use your newfound Bash powers to automate the app's Workspace (which, if you recall from Where Work is Done on page 7 is where *your app* is automated and managed). CatSay does this via `bin/setup` and `bin/run`.

Of note, however, is that because the Workspace can rely on software having been installed (thanks to the Foundational Core), `bin/setup` (or whatever other automation your app needs) can use the programming language and tools of your choice and not Bash. Nice!

Don't forget that you don't have do `dx/exec bin/setup`, you could `dx/exec bash` and then run commands on a command line:

```
your-computer> dx/exec bash
inside-the-container> bin/setup
«output»
inside-the-container> bin/test
«output»
inside-the-container> bin/run
«output»
```

But Wait, There's More

With what we've just gone through, you can use what we built as your dev environment. Or, you can use Docker and Bash to make one that works the way you want. With an understanding of how Docker works, what is called what, and how to wield bash, you can create powerful, usable tools that have *very* few dependencies.

One thing that's worth discussing is how to customize this to your or your team's needs. When you run `dx/exec bash` you will not have any of your specialized aliases or configuration.

13

Customizing Your Dev Environment

A complex and flexible dev environment is invariably found to have evolved from a simple dev environment that worked. The inverse proposition also appears to be true: A complex dev environment designed from scratch never works and cannot be made to work. You have to start over, beginning with a working simple dev environment. Though, you know what, now that I think about it, flexible and complex dev environments don't work either. "Systems", am I right?

—*John Gall on Dev Environments*

A key to sustainability is consistency. And consistency means reducing flexibility, customizations, and configuration. Some teams go so far as to prescribe a single editor for all work. That might be a bit extreme, but we should still talk about how to add some configurability to what we've just built.

Before we get into it, please consider what you are configuring and why. The more customized the dev environment, the more ways it can break, the more complicated it will be to maintain, and the more likely you will need to fall back on out-of-date documentation.

Remember that we learned and built all this to avoid complexity. Remember that you are building a dev environment for your app and your team only—you aren't building a generic dev-environment-as-a-service startup.

With that sermon out of the way, there are two techniques that can help provide some level of customization:

- Customize workflows through automation and integration of `dx/exec` into your existing Workspace.
- Modify `dx/build` to allow developers to inject configuration into their images.

13.1 Customize Workflows Via Scripts and Aliases on Your Host

This technique boils down to "don't run `bash` in the container". This is the technique I use most of the time. Because I rarely "log in" to the dev container, I don't miss my dotfiles that aren't a part of it. To make this work, you have to make it so you don't *need* to log in to the container.

CatSay's `bin/setup` is an example of a way to make this work—it scripts the app setup, so only need to run `dx/exec bin/setup`. If there are commonly-needed tasks such as loading dev data, running tests, or creating new code structures, the best way to manage them is by creating scripts.

Some frameworks like Rails provide direct support for automation scripts. But, pretty much every programming language has a library for building command-line apps. I guarantee you they are all better than `getopts`, which, we have effectively used to build a great user experience.

That said, stuff like changing directories, listing files, or any other command-line activity can't always be put into a script. Since most file management you perform on your computer will be reflected inside the container, much of your existing workflows will continue to work. The only changes are tasks that require interacting with the app that now have to be run inside the container.

If your editor is configurable, you should be able to make project-specific editor configuration to use `dx/exec`. For example, if you have Control-R set to run your tests via `bin/tests`, you should be able to configure your editor to run `dx/exec bin/tests`. My editor—vim—can do this, and it was created 1988 based on an editor created in 1976. Certainly, your editor of choice can be configured as well.

For execution outside your editor, an alias like `de` could be created to prepend `dx/exec`:

```
alias de=dx/exec
```

Then, you can type `de bin/setup` to run `dx/exec bin/setup`. You could even make `de` a function that checks for the existence of `dx/exec` and, if it's not found, run the command normally. This would allow you to work with both Docker-based and host-based projects.

Although typing a few extra characters may not seem like much, it can add up. We all have only so many keystrokes in us, and some of us start off with many fewer available. A way to manage this with our Docker-based setup would be to create the same shortcuts and aliases inside the container as we have outside of it.

13.2 Adding Your Own Files to the Image

Because our dev images are just for local dev and not for production, we aren't sharing the images with other developers (or deploying them to servers). This means that if we were to allow the images to be customized, it's not going to cause a problem for anyone else. The trick to making this sustainable is to provide a file where developers' customizations can live, so they don't have to directly edit `Dockerfile.dev`.

When we looked at Redis' `Dockerfile` on page 53, it used the `COPY` directive to copy files from a Redis maintainers' computer into the Docker image. We can use that technique to solve this problem.

`COPY` is quite flexible, so I'll show a basic example of how you could allow minimal injection of custom behavior. We'll create a convention that the file `.bashrc.dx.local` contains developer-specific Bash customization. This file is expected to be in the root of your app and is *not* something you check into version control. It is also optional.

We'll copy this file into the image and then modify `~/.bashrc` so that it sources this file (since there may be a `~/.bashrc` file already). Note that `COPY` cannot use `~` to reference the user's home directory, so we must use the full path, `/root/`.

In `Dockerfile.dev`, we'll add this toward the end:

```
# Dockerfile.dev

  #              the right way to update Bundler :)
  RUN gem install bundler

→ # Copy developer-specific Bash configuration into the image
→ COPY .bashrc.dx.local /root/.bashrc.dx.local
→ # Modify the existing /root/.bashrc to source the customizations
→ RUN echo "# Dev-specific Bash customizations" >> ~/.bashrc && \
→     echo ". ./.bashrc.dx.local" >> ~/.bashrc
  # Source code will be available here
  WORKDIR /root/catsay
```

Note that the `RUN` directive is using `>>` which concatenates text to the end of a file, creating that file if it exists. A lot of times, `~/.bashrc` already exists and we don't want to overwrite it. Also note that we add a comment about what's happening before using `.` to source the `.bashrc.dx.local` file that we copied via the `COPY` directive.

`COPY` requires that the file it's copying exist, but we want this file to be optional. We can take advantage of what we've built to inject further behavior. Since `dx/build` is a protocol for creating the Foundational Core (which we discussed in "Scripts as Protocols for Future Enhancements" on page 61), we can enhance it to handle this new requirement.

Let's change it so that it ensures `.bashrc.dx.local` exists. If it doesn't, we'll create a blank one that contains a comment explaining the purpose of the file. We'll also make sure it's listed in `.gitignore` so that it doesn't get checked into version control.

This will use what we've learned already about Bash plus one new thing. `[` accepts `-e «file»` as an argument to check if `«file»` exists. We can use this to check if `.bashrc.dx.local` exists:

```
if [ -e .bashrc.dx.local ]; then
  echo "the file exists"
else
  echo "the file does not exist"
fi
```

To check if `.bashrc.dx.local` is in the `.gitignore` file, we'll use `grep`. `grep` exits 0 if the string you give it is found inside the file you give it. It exits nonzero if the string is not found. `grep` does produce output, so we'll use some previously-learned symbol soup to direct all that output to `dev/null`.

```
if grep .bashrc.dx.local .gitignore > /dev/null 2>&1; then
  echo "it's in the file"
else
  echo "it's not in the file
fi
```

Given all that, here's the code, including liberal use of `log` to let the user know what's going on:

```
# dx/build

  shift $((OPTIND -1))

  check_for_docker
→ BASHRC_LOCAL="${ROOT_DIR}"/.bashrc.dx.local
→
→ if [ -e "${BASHRC_LOCAL}" ]; then
→   log "${BASHRC_LOCAL} exists - not touching it"
→ else
→   log "${BASHRC_LOCAL} missing - creating"
→   echo "# Place custom Bash configuration to use" >> "${BASHRC_LOCAL}"
→   echo "# inside the running container here"      >> "${BASHRC_LOCAL}"
→ fi
→ if grep "${BASHRC_LOCAL}" .gitignore > /dev/null 2>&1; then
→   log "${BASHRC_LOCAL} is already being ignored"
→ else
→   log "${BASHRC_LOCAL} is not being ignored. Adding to .gitignore"
→   echo "# This is for developer-specific customizations" >> .gitignore
→   echo "${BASHRC_LOCAL}" >> .gitignore
→ fi
```

```
  log "Building Docker image '${IMAGE}'"
  docker build \
```

Before creating our own `.bashrc.dx.local`, let's run the script as it is to make sure it works in the default case:

```
> dx/build
«lots of output»
```

Great! Now, let's add a single alias to the file so we can see it become available in the image. We'll alias `ll` to run `ls -l`, which is a pretty common alias people use.

```
# .bashrc.dx.local

alias ll='ls -l'
```

In case you are running the dev environment from a previous chapter, let's stop it:

```
> dx/stop
[ dx/stop ] Docker is installed!
[ dx/stop ] Stopping dev environment
[ dx/stop ] Dev environment stopped
```

Now, we'll rebuild our image:

```
> dx/build
[ dx/build ] Docker is installed!
[ dx/build ] /root/work/catsay/.bashrc.dx.local exists - not. . .
[ dx/build ] /root/work/catsay/.bashrc.dx.local is already b. . .
[ dx/build ] Building Docker image 'catsay-dev:debian-12.1'
sha256:094ac216a534701f00feeab599b8c3be4d05cbd872fb9e3a7ed69. . .
[ dx/build ] Docker image 'catsay-dev:debian-12.1' is built
```

The new image should contain our `.bashrc.dx.local` copied to `/root/`. Let's start everything up:

```
> dx/start
[ dx/start ] Docker is installed!
[ dx/start ] Starting dev environment
 Network catsay_default  Creating
 Network catsay_default  Created
 Container catsay-app-1  Creating
 Container catsay-redis-1  Creating
```

```
 Container catsay-app-1  Created
 Container catsay-redis-1  Created
 Container catsay-app-1  Starting
 Container catsay-redis-1  Starting
 Container catsay-app-1  Started
 Container catsay-redis-1  Started
[ dx/start ] Dev environment started
```

Now, you can run `dx/exec bash`, and then `ll` should be available:

```
> dx/exec bash
root@bd4237a42b0b:~/catsay# ll
total 44
-rw-r--r-- 1 root root   595 Feb  1 22:16 Dockerfile.dev
-rw-r--r-- 1 root root   534 Feb  1 22:16 Gemfile
-rw-r--r-- 1 root root  1463 Feb  1 22:16 Gemfile.lock
-rw-r--r-- 1 root root   567 Feb  1 22:16 README.md
-rw-r--r-- 1 root root   231 Feb  1 22:16 Rakefile
drwxr-xr-x 6 root root   192 Feb  1 22:16 app
drwxr-xr-x 7 root root   224 Feb  1 22:16 bin
-rw-r--r-- 1 root root   281 Feb  1 22:17 docker-compose.dev.yml
drwxr-xr-x 8 root root   256 Feb  1 22:17 dx
drwxr-xr-x 8 root root   256 Feb  1 22:16 node_modules
-rw-r--r-- 1 root root 12409 Feb  1 22:17 package-lock.json
-rw-r--r-- 1 root root   334 Feb  1 22:16 package.json
drwxr-xr-x 3 root root    96 Feb  1 22:16 test
drwxr-xr-x 3 root root    96 Feb  1 22:16 tmp
```

This is just an example of what you can do. You can could use this technique in other ways. For example, you could support a file named, say, `install-additional-tools.sh` that is copied into the image and executed. This file could be filled with developer-specific tooling installation. Or, you could use `COPY` to place secrets or API keys you need inside the container. Since the images you build won't be pushed to DockerHub, it's generally safe[1].

All of this shows you the power of thinking of our scripts as protocols. If we had additional customizations we wanted to make that didn't find into the build step, we have `dx/start`, `dx/stop`, and `dx/exec` available as parts of that protocol.

Up Next

At this point, we have *created* a dev environment, and you now know all that you need to, in order to create one for just about any project. All told, we don't have that much code to maintain. But maintain it, we must.

[1]There is not enough space in this book to get into the nuances of a) having secrets you need in development, and b) putting them into an image that is one command-line invocation away from being pushed up to the public Internet. Be careful and make sure you have a documented (or automated) way to disable secrets and quickly generate new ones.

The next chapter is going to deal with how to maintain this system over time. We'll cover debugging this when you need to make changes as well as managing the Docker images and feeling confident that the Bash scripts are working.

14

Sustainably Maintaining The Dev Environment

I have a poor freezingly cold drive
So far from where I need all the bytes.
Scavenging through the drive's constant lulls
So far from where I must have all the bytes.
Wish I knew the way to reach the images I love
There is no way
Wish I had the command-line prowess to attract the images I love.
But you see, I've got no Bash skills

—*Stephen Patrick Morrissey, Seasick, Yet Still Running Docker*

There are a few issues that are worth discussing based on what we've just done:

- How can Dockerfiles be debugged?
- How do we manage the various Docker images taking up space on our computers?
- Can we test the Bash scripts?

14.1 Debugging

In "Establish a Chain of Trust for Software Installation" on page 30, we learned how to find the set of instructions to install software into our image. During the writing of this book, those instructions changed a few times. I found out because things didn't work and I had to debug them. Let's talk about some techniques for doing that.

The three techniques I've used for understanding failures in my Dockerfile are:

- Split up long command-line invocations to find out where the problem lies.
- *Carefully* search the Internet for answers.
- Run a base image and test installation commands manually.

When I was first using Docker, I'd often have a hard time figuring out exactly what went wrong. This is where splitting up long command lines can help

14.1.1 Split up Command Line Invocations

In an earlier version of the book, I was using a pipeline to install NodeJS. It looked like so:

```
RUN curl -fsSL https://deb.nodesource.com/setup_20.x | bash - && \
    apt-get install -y nodejs
```

As mentioned before, if `curl` fails, `bash` will still be run. This caused an older version of NodeJS to be installed, and the Docker image was successfully built. I didn't remember to `set -o pipefail`.

I was able to figure out what happened by temporarily splitting up the command line invocation into separate steps and `RUN` directives:

```
RUN curl -fsSL https://deb.nodesource.com/setup_20.x > /tmp/node20.out
RUN cat /tmp/mode20.out | bash -
RUN apt-get install -y nodejs
```

Doing this, the first `RUN` directive clearly failed since `curl` was not installed. Of course, when I looked back at the original failure, there *was* a message that `curl` was not installed, but it was buried in reams of other extraneous output and I just missed it.

Even though you don't want three layers, temporarily splitting them up can help figure out exactly where things are going wrong.

If splitting up the command line doesn't lead to a solution, it usually leads to a better error message you can search for. But, you have to be careful in doing so.

14.1.2 Careful Internet Searching is a lot Different than Googling

A common issue when searching the Internet for technical information is finding information that was relevant for an older version of the software you are using, but is either out of date or no longer the best practice. This phenomenon has only been exacerbated with the arrival of AI chatbots that may have only been trained on older information.

That said, most answers to problems you have are out there. You are not a unique snowflake and are probably doing something pretty common that someone else has run into. This is why using standard, commonly-used tools is a good thing.

Search for the Exact Error Message

If `apt-get install -yq postgresql` is giving you this error:

```
download failed
Oracle JDK 7 is NOT installed.
dpkg: error processing package oracle-java7-installer (--configure):
 subprocess installed post-installation script returned error exit status 1
Errors were encountered while processing:
 oracle-java7-installer
E: Sub-process /usr/bin/dpkg returned an error code (1)
```

Don't search for "apt can't install postgres". Search for the part of that error that seems most specific, for example "error processing package oracle-java7-installer (–configure)". You are using common tools, and so your errors should be common. And most search engines are smart enough to lead you to links that are close to your error message if you can't find it exactly.

The two most useful sites for results are Stack Overflow and GitHub.

How to Interpret Stack Overflow Answers

Stack Overflow has a lot of out-of-date answers. But they are often answers to questions that are still relevant. When you see a question that appears to be related to your problem, read more than just the green-checked answer.

Often, the second or third highest-rated answer is newer and more appropriate for the version of whatever software you are using. If these answers aren't quite right, read the tiny comments attached to each answer. I have found insights and other links in those comments that have solved my problem.

The key is to examine the timestamp of everything to see what is most recent or at least more up to date. GitHub issues works similarly.

GitHub Issues can be a Treasure Trove

Because Docker is so ubiquitous, you may find GitHub Issues describing the same problem you are having, but on some random unrelated piece of software. Often, a user of the software is trying to set it up via Docker and having some problem.

If that software uses the same underlying language or tools as your app, the discussion in the issue can often be extremely helpful. Because GitHub issues are ordered by date, you may need to do a lot of scrolling and skimming. I have definitely found helpful answers way toward the bottom of an Issues page.

Often, comments will link to other Issues or Pull Requests, even to other repos. Follow these and you can sometimes find an answer.

I've solved almost every Docker problem I've had by Stack Overflow or GitHub issues. Blogs and AI Chatbots, however, are trickier.

Beware AI Chatbots and Blog Posts

AI Chatbots are notoriously unreliable, confidently creating solutions out of thin air that don't work at all. This is partly due to their nature, but also due to the recency of their training data. ChatGPT can't answer a question about the latest release of Postgres if it hasn't been fed anything since Postgres was released.

Blog posts by random people can be similarly unreliable. They are often the equivalent of seeing a Stack Overflow question with only the top-rated answer and no other comments. And many people just don't put a date on their blog posts. I don't get it.

This isn't to say that you should ignore what AI Chatbots or blog posts tell you. You can always try them to see if they work. But, if they don't, you should not read too much into that. Don't be tempted to think the AI was on the right track. I can assure you, it is not.

No matter how you get solutions, you will have to try them out, and doing so by editing the Dockerfile and re-running `docker build` can be tedious. I find it useful to execute commands I'm debugging inside the base image directly.

14.1.3 Try Commands Against a Base Image

If you have a base image, you can often try out solutions by running against that base image, or running against the image built before the first error.

For example, if you were having problems with NodeJS, you could comment out everything in `Dockerfile.dev` starting from that invocation:

```
FROM debian:12.1

RUN apt-get update --quiet --yes

# From https://www.ruby-lang.org/en/documentation/installation/#apt
# NOTE: build-essential is needed to install C extensions
# NOTE: curl is needed to install Node
RUN apt-get install --quiet --yes ruby-full build-essential curl

# Based on
# https://github.com/nodesource/distributions?tab=readme-ov-file#us. . .
→ #RUN curl -fsSL https://deb.nodesource.com/setup_22.x -o node_setup.sh && \
→ #    bash node_setup.sh && \
→ #    apt-get install --quiet --yes nodejs
«etc»
```

Now, when you `dx/build`, the image should build successfully, and you can `dx/start`, then `dx/exec bash` to log in to the image. From there you can run commands directly to try things out to see if they are working. The commands you run this way are run the exact same way when running `dx/build` (i.e. `docker` build). Thus, if you find a solution that works when executed in a shell inside your image, it should work from the Dockerfile as well.

14.1.4 Verifying Your Solution

It's really important to verify your solution by finding documentation. Often, a fix can appear to work, but not really solve the problem at hand, or solve it in an unsustainable way.

What I like to do is, when I have a set of commands that works, go to the vendor or app's documentation and read about the commands I'm running. I will find documentation on the various flags I'm using and arguments I've giving.

As I mentioned with getopts, I would've never figured that out without Stack Overflow, but I was able to then read Bash's documentation and see exactly why each part of the solution was needed and what purpose it served. You should do this, too.

If possible, leave a link to what you've found, or update the comment to indicate why the RUN directive is the way it is. This will be useful for debugging later.

14.2 Managing Your Docker Install

Go ahead and run docker image ls. You might not see much if this book is your first time using Docker. Or, you might see a ton of stuff. And you may want to clean it up from time to time.

You can see how much disk space all your images are taking up via docker system df:

```
> docker system df
TYPE            TOTAL     ACTIVE    SIZE      RECLAIMABLE
Images          34        23        28.63GB   17.93GB (62%)
Containers      38        7         874.9MB   722.7MB (82%)
Local Volumes   20        12        1.697GB   1.186GB (69%)
Build Cache     261       0         1.582GB   1.582GB
```

Like all Docker commands, this one isn't well documented and somewhat misleading. The space under the SIZE heading should be accurate. This is the output from my computer and it seems correct that I'm currently using almost 30 gigabytes of space for Docker images. It's that RECLAIMABLE part that is misleading.

Docker considers an image reclaimable if no running container is using it. You may have containers from other projects that aren't running now, but that you'd like to be able to run later. In that case, you don't want to reclaim that image. But, even if you did, it's not easy to figure out which images are reclaimable.

You can try to run docker image ls, but this won't show you which are reclaimable. You can try to delete images that look like you don't need them by running docker image rm, but you'll usually see a message like this:

```
> docker image rm fd79cb10f4de
Error response from daemon: conflict: unable to
delete fd79cb10f4de (must be forced) - image
is being used by stopped container 29b949f79ac4
```

To make matters even worse, if you run `docker container ls`, you often won't see the referenced container (the `29b949f79ac4` in this case). `docker container ls` only shows *running* containers by default. It's almost like Docker doesn't want you to actually reclaim bytes from your own internal storage.

Docker's terminology on page \pageref{chapter-what-is-docker, along with Docker's tagging system on page 24 makes this make sense. Containers need images to be able to start and so even a stopped container could use that image. Deleting the image would make it impossible to start the container. Further, every time we build an image, that image is named, which leaves any previously-built image un-named, and thus reclaimable.

This is all shown in the figure "Dangling and Reclaimable Images" on page 112. Image A is referenced by two stopped containers, so it's considered reclaimable, but not dangling. You cannot remove it without removing the containers. Image B is similar, except its container is running, so it's *not* reclaimable. Image C, however, can be removed, but it's not dangling since it has a name referencing it. Image D has no such name. It's just a lonely image, sitting around taking up space.

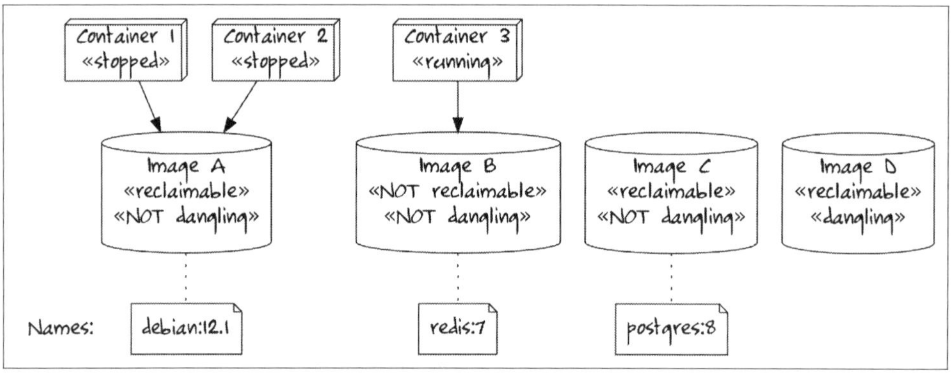

Figure 14.1: Dangling and Reclaimable Images

You can't really list images that are reclaimable, but you can distinguish dangling from not using the `--filter` option to `docker image ls`:

```
docker image ls --filter "dangling=true"
```

You can delete those images with `docker image prune`. You can delete both dangling *and* any reclaimable image not being used by a container via `docker image prune -a`. To prune *all* reclaimable images, you must prune all stopped containers via `docker container prune`, then `docker image prune` or `docker image prune -a`.

In general, `docker container prune` is safe to run because `dx/start` (which uses `docker compose`) will recreate any needed containers when it's next asked to start up the dev environment. `docker image prune` is safe, since it will remove images that you are extremely unlikely to need.

`docker image prune -a`, however, is less safe, since Docker doesn't provide repeatable builds. Ideally, this won't matter to your app, because you chose tags appropriate for what you are working on. For example, it should not matter if today we are using NodeJS 22.1 and tomorrow we are using 22.2. "Should" and "Ideally" aren't the basis for great technical strategies, however.

The best way to manage this is to frequently update your images. For example, every Monday you could start your week with `dx/build`, then re-run your app's test suite. By doing updates frequently, the changes from update-to-update won't be drastic, and you will be able to figure out what is the cause of any trouble, if any.

That mostly covers maintaining your Docker-related infrastructure, but what about the Bash scripts? Can we make sure they are working in some way?

14.3 Quality-control of Bash Scripts

Testing command-line scripts is notoriously difficult. The commands can have irreversible effects on a computer, and assertions can be complicated. There are three techniques that, when used in conjunction, can give you a sense of the quality of your scripts without having to maintain brittle tests.

- Running these scripts every day will ensure they are working. You will be running `dx/build` weekly, and `dx/start` daily, and `dx/exec` many times per day. You will know if they are broken and can fix them. You'll have to.
- Use these scripts as part of your continuous integration system. Since `dx/build` is used to create the dev environment, and `dx/exec` is used to execute all automation, those can be the basis if your continuous integration scripting. This will tell you if the scripts are working without having to run them locally, *and* provide a forcing-function to keep them working, since you can't deploy if they are broken.
- Run `shellcheck`[1] on the scripts and address what it says. `shellcheck` is a static analyzer for Bash scripts that identifies bugs, dangerous constructs, and other code you should avoid. Here's what it says about `dx/exec`:

```
> shellcheck dx/exec
In dx/exec line 54:
log "Executing '${@}' inside container with service named '${SERVICE}'"
              ^--^ SC2145 (error): Argument mixes string and array.
                                   Use * or separate argument.

For more information:
  https://www.shellcheck.net/wiki/SC2145 -- Argument mixes string
                                             and array. ...
```

[1] https://www.shellcheck.net

If you go to that referenced page, you will learn a lot about Bash! In this case, the data type of `${@}` is actually an array, and the behavior of an array when interpolated inside a string is not defined. Changing it to use `${*}`, which is not an array, produces predictable behavior in this case.

`shellcheck` is full of useful stuff like this. I learned a lot about Bash by using `shellcheck`.

Almost Done

Before we complete this journey, I want to address a few downsides to what we have and how to manage those.

15 There's No Such Thing as a Free Lunch

> *So you think that static typing is the root of all evil? Have you ever asked what is the root of static typing? Static typing is a tool of exchange, which can't exist unless there are values to store and programs to store them. Static typing is the material shape of the principle that programs who wish to deal with one another must deal by types and give isomorphism for isomorphism. Static typing is not the tool of the Ruby hipsters, who claim productivity by happiness, or of the React Bros, who take it from you by force. Static typing is made possible only by the computer science researchers who produce papers. Is this what you consider evil?*
>
> *—Another insufferable pedant on Hacker News*

There are three downsides we should discuss: poor I/O performance, processor architecture issues, and impedance mismatches with production images.

15.1 Suboptimal I/O Performance on Some Non-Linux Platforms

If your computer is a Linux computer, Docker works well, and I/O performance should be good. This is because Docker on Linux isn't running a virtual machine. Julia Evans' delightful 'zine How Containers Work[1] will give you an overview of this, if you are interested.

On a Mac, Docker is implemented as a virtual machine. This means that the volume we mounted containing our source code must go through an emulation layer. This means it's slower than it would be on Linux. As of a few years ago, this performance gap was pretty big. But, with the introduction of virtiofs[2], this gap has narrowed significantly.

That said, there are other issues that can come up if you are using tools based on evented I/O. Webpack is an example of something that uses this. When you

[1] https://wizardzines.com/zines/containers/

[2] https://www.docker.com/blog/speed-boost-achievement-unlocked-on-docker-desktop-4-6-for-mac/

instruct Webpack to watch your `.js` files for changes, it will use the operating system's filesystem to register for events. The OS will send it events when files change, so it can know to rebuild your JS bundle.

The filesystem used in our volume mount on Mac (or Windows) doesn't support these events. In Webpack's case, it means that the feature just silently never does anything[3]. Instead, you must configure *polling*, where Webpack will explicitly examine the filesystem for changes.

Docker's use for dev environments is common enough that most tools do document stuff like this, but you need to be aware of it. Any auto-watcher or other tool that rebuilds your app when files change needs to work based on polling.

When coupled with the performance gap regarding I/O performance, this does mean that a very large app could be slower to rebuild when run inside a Docker container. How much slower depends on the app and the tooling you have chosen. And, the amount of slowness may not actually matter that much.

One place where slowness can be introduced if you aren't careful is when you run an image with the wrong processor architecture.

15.2 Processor Architecture Issues AKA Docker Platform

You may be using an Intel-based Linux box. Or, you might be on a shiny new Apple Silicon Mac. I didn't give you any real instructions related to this because it's not generally an issue. But it can be.

If you go back to the Debian DockerHub page[4] and scroll down a bit, you'll see a section titled "Quick Reference (cont.)", and there is a bullet there labeled "Supported Architectures". If you then click more info[5], you'll see a page where Docker is trying to describe what's going on.

Docker has a concept called "Multi-platform images", sometimes called "multi-arch images". When Debian builds their image, they will arrange for it to be built across many different platforms. Those strings, such as "amd64" or "i386" are the names of *platforms*, which represent specific processor architectures.

These multi-platform images allow Docker to use the appropriate image for the host, i.e. your computer. When I run `dx/build` and `dx/start` on my Apple Silicon mac, I'll get images built for that platform (which is confusingly named "arm64"). If you are running an Intel-based Linux box, those same commands will use images built for the equally-confusingly-named "amd64" platform.

Where problems arise is if you are using an image that is *not* multi platform. In this case, usually the image is only built for the "amd64" platform, and anyone on your team with an Apple Silicon-based mac will have issues. Docker on Apple Silicon is willing to try to run an amd64-based image, and it kinda works.

[3]One of the many reasons to avoid Webpack if you can. Many tools actually tell you when what you ask them to do isn't working, and those are good tools.

[4]https://hub.docker.com/_/debian

[5]https://github.com/docker-library/official-images#architectures-other-than-amd64

It does this via emulation that is slow (due to emulation just being slow) and flaky (due to the emulator not supporting every feature of the processor its emulating). This means it'll take you a long time to realize something is wrong.

It's not easy to figure out if your image supports your architecture. One way to attempt to figure it out is to run `docker buildx imagetools inspect «image name»`. This command[6] is effectively undocumented if you don't know how multi-platform images are built. In the output of this command, you will a list of *manifests*. If you see one that has your platform next to `Platform:` that is a strong indicator this image was built for your platform.

Another way to check is to pull the image from Docker Hub and use `docker image inspect`. For example, if you tried `docker buildx imagetools inspect postgres:8`, you won't see anything about manifests. You can download that image by running `docker image pull postgres:8`. Once that's done, run `docker image ls` to get the SHA of the image you downloaded. Then do `docker image inspect «SHA»`.

That command will dump out a ton of JSON, but somewhere in that big huge wall of text you will see the key `"Architecture"` and its value will be the platform that image was built for. In this case, that's "amd64", which means an Intel processor and that won't really work on Apple Silicon. If you do the exact same thing for `postgres:9`, and you are on Apple Silicon, you will see that the image's `Architecture` is `arm64`.

This is a lot, and generally, if you are using up-to-date, supported tools, you will get an image built for your platform. But if something seems really slow or buggy, checking the platform of the image is a place to start.

15.3 Production/Dev Mismatches

Containers for production have a different set of goals than we have for dev. Production containers need to be small, and have as little software on them as possible. Dev containers need whatever they need, and size isn't that much of a concern.

Further, production containers will usually target a single processor architecture, whereas your dev team might have a mix of Apple Silicon, Intel, AMD, or whatever. As we just discussed, Docker will do its best to pull an image built for your computer's architecture.

This means there will naturally be a mismatch with what is running in production and what is running on dev. The main bulwark against this is to run your continuous integration test suite using the production architecture. How you arrange this depends on your chosen CI tool. You will need to make sure that where you are running CI—and thus where you are running `dx/build`—is the same operating system and processor as on production.

One last downside is that there are tech companies trying to provide you a dev environment toolchain that will likely save you some time up-front at the cost of ceding ownership of your core competency.

[6] https://docs.docker.com/engine/reference/commandline/buildx_imagetools_inspect/

16

Tech Companies Should Not Own Your Dev Environment

> *You don't know what hard times are, daddy. Hard times are when the journalists around this country are out of work, they got 4 or 5 kids and can't get them a new iPad, can't buy them a ticket to see Taylor. Hard times are when the product designers are out of work and they tell 'em go home. And hard times are when a senior engineer has worked at a job for thirty years, thirty years, and they give them an Amazon gift card, kick 'em in the butt and say "hey a large language model took your place, son", that's hard times! That's hard times!*
>
> —*Dusty Rhodes, Former Open AI Board Member*

I promise this is only a *partial* rant. This chapter is encouraging you to own your own tools, and outlines my thinking about why, especially when there are many tech companies that want to provide you a shiny solution whose landing page is full of big fonts and smooth animations.

Essentially, your dev environment is a core competency that you must own. This means you must control it and understand it. If you do this, you don't need some tech company's convoluted product.

16.1 What is a Core Competency?

A core competency is knowledge and skills you must have or acquire that are fundamental to your ability to, in this context, write software. If your app is built on Ruby on Rails, then knowing Ruby on Rails—and therefore Ruby—is a core competency. This also implies that SQL, HTML, and CSS are also core competencies. You must either already understand them or be able to learn them. You cannot outsource them.

A counter-example would be memory management. Ruby takes care of that and you don't *need* to have a deep understanding of how it works. You may need to know it a bit, but you can merrily write and ship apps with Ruby on Rails and never have to know this.

To maintain focus and be productive, it's common to own your core competencies and outsource everything else. The thinking is that whatever you need to know to be productive, you must be in control of—to avoid losing the ability to work—but let someone else handle everything the other stuff.

What I believe is that your dev environment is a core competency.

16.2 Your Dev Environment is Your Core Competency

Without a dev environment, you literally cannot do development. That's the definition of a dev environment. While a dev environment is comprised of several pieces (that we discussed in A Dev Environment Defined on page 7), all of it must be functional for you to do work.

This means that if you are unable to set up your operating system, or unable to install and configure the tools you need to write, test, and run your app, you are a pretty high risk of getting into a situation where you can't do any work. This effect is most commonly seen with inexperienced developers who, naturally, have not learned any of this yet.

When they hit a problem, they have no idea what to do, because they don't have any conception of what the parts of their dev environment even are, much less how to figure out what aspects are broken. Hopefully, they have caring and experienced engineers to level them up and get them able to do work.

But what if *you* are ~~Pagliacci~~ the most experienced? What if you have no one to turn to? You'll have to figure it out. And when you do, do you want to figure out something you and your team built, based on commonly-available tools, or do you want to dig into something someone else made that you have no way to deeply examine?

For something as vital as your dev environment—the thing that allows you to even do work—the answer is that you do not want to debug or maintain something you cannot control. Your dev environment should be a core competency, at least your *team's* core competency, if not every single members'.

16.3 But Microsoft Has an Open Source Spec About Exactly This!

You may use Visual Studio Code to do your work. It's currently quite popular and it supports something called The Dev Containers Spec[1]. I would encourage you to read the "spec" and tell me how enlightened it makes you feel. I have read it several times and cannot make head or tail of it.

You may also have heard of a company called "Jetpack" that make something called DevBox[2]. It claims you will own your dev environment because it's based on open source tools that you also don't have to know. I would encourage you to examine those tools and decide how much you trust that you won't have to know them. Hint: try to find their support page.

It may seem enticing to outsource your dev environment—something I've gone to great pains to demonstrate is complex—to a huge experienced company like

[1] https://containers.dev
[2] https://jetpack.io/devbox

Microsoft, or a hungry, dedicated startup like Jetpack. For anything that's not a core competency, I would agree. But not a core competency.

There are two major risks with letting some other company own your dev environment. The first is that they aren't going to support you and your teams' needs. Do you honestly think Microsoft are going to help you figure out why your free copy of VS Code isn't working with some library you needed to install? And Jetpack don't even have a way to take your money for support. You did try to find their support page, right? It's not there.

This means if anything goes wrong with these tools, you are on your own. You'll need to look under the hood and understand the technology these tools are built on so you can then try to solve your problem. This leads to the second major risk, which is that generalized tools are, by their nature, extremely complex.

Jetpack's DevBox uses Nix under the hood. Their Nix installation script for NodeJS is 200+ lines of code that you can view on GitHub[3]. I'm not sure if this is a testament to Nix, but Microsoft's DevContainers NodeJS "feature" requires double that—over 400 lines of Bash[4].

Remember that we installed NodeJS using the instructions provided by the NodeJS team. It required two lines of code. Granted, it only works for Debian Linux, but that's all we need it to work for. It's not hard to debug.

If your install of DevBox fails to install NodeJS, let's be real. You are not gonna want to learn Nix and then dig into that 200 line set of instructions to figure out what went wrong. And Jetpack have no obligation to help you—they have ceded that burden with the claim that the tool is open source.

Just because a tool is open source doesn't mean it's comprehensible. I'm sure both Jetpack and Microsoft have good reasons for writing their installation instructions the way they do, but coupling your very means of production to them—especially given how easy it is to manage yourself—is not a wise trade-off.

16.4 Hold Up, isn't Docker Also Some Tech Company That Doesn't Care About Me?

It is true that Docker is a privately-held, likely-unprofitable, venture-backed company. They will take your money for support[5] at least, but Docker aren't going to debug what you put in your Dockerfiles any more than Microsoft will help you craft the perfect 40 lines of JSON for your devcontainer.

But consider that Docker is extremely widely used and has been around for years. DevBox is based on Nix, which is extremely niche and generally unloved. Also consider that Docker exists almost entirely to provide the tools we've been using and to manage the container registry where we get our images. Microsoft makes most of their money from Windows, Azure, and Word.

[3]https://github.com/NixOS/nixpkgs/blob/master/pkgs/development/web/nodejs/nodejs.nix
[4]https://github.com/devcontainers/features/blob/main/src/node/install.sh
[5]https://www.docker.com/pricing/

To say all this another way, if you agree that you should own your core competencies, and that your dev environment is one such thing, you would be well-served by constructing your dev environment using reliable, stable, widely-understood technologies. Docker and Bash fit that bill. If worst comes to worst, you can easily pay for Docker or Bash expertise.

On the other hand, if you really do think that Microsoft or some startup should be providing you and your team their dev environment automation tools, primarily I'd like to remind you that there are no refunds for this book. Secondly, however, you really do need to commit to learning the underlying open source tools upon which these companies' offerings are built. This will have a cost and it won't be one you'll be happy to pay, especially since you won't be able to control when the bill comes due.

In The End There Was Still The Command Line

This brings us to the end! You now know a lot more about Docker, you know how to find reliable images to base your dev environment on or to run ancillary services. You also leveled-up on your Bash programming! You have the power to make user-friendly Bash scripts!

The bigger picture of what you should take away from all this is that you should automate your dev environment. You should control it and know how it works, and design it to allow the flexibility developers want—editor and hardware—without the flexibility they don't need—OS.

Automating your dev environment is within grasp of even the smallest team. Now get after it!

A

The Docker Lexicon for Regular People

"Forget about it" is like if you agree with someone, you know, like Perl was great before version 5, forget about it. But then, if you disagree, like functional programming is better than imperative? Forget about it! You know? But then, it's also like if something's the greatest thing in the world, like Ruby on Rails 3.0, forget about it. But it's also like saying go to hell, too. Like, you know, like "Hey Patty, your cohort in that A/B test tanked our conversion rate" and Patty says "Forget about it!". Sometimes, it just means forget about it.

—Donald "Joe" Brasco "Pistone", former Fog Creek Staff Engineer

Table A.1: Docker Nouns

Docker	English
Container	Virtual Computer
Container Registry	Hosted Images
Dockerfile	Image Build Script
Host	Your Computer
Image	Disk Image for a Virtual Computer
Port	Network Port on a Virtual Computer
Repository	Remote location for different versions of the same image
Volume	Disk

Table A.2: Docker Verbs

Docker	English
build (an image)	Create an image from a Dockerfile
create (a container)	Order a computer from Amazon and put a hard drive in it when it shows up
expose (a port)	Allow another container to access a port in this container
mount (a volume)	Make a disk available

Docker	English
pull (an image)	Fetch an image from a remote registry and store it for later use
publish (a port)	Map a container's port to your computer's port on `localhost`
push (an image)	Send an image to a remote registry
start (a container)	Turn on a computer
stop (a container)	Shut down a computer

B

Bash and Command-Line Quick Reference

Ready are you? What know you of ready? Through eight rounds of investment have I trained UNIX hackers. My own counsel I will keep on who is to be trained. A UNIX hacker must have the deepest commitment, the most serious mind. React? Hmph. Mobile Apps? Heh. A UNIX hacker craves not these things.

—OH at the bar of Pied Piper, Palace Hotel, San Francisco

B.1 Concepts

Environment, or "UNIX Environment" A set of keys and values that a process can access when it executes. The UNIX Environment is a common way to pass complex information from one process to the next. Each key/value pair is called an *Environment Variable*. Both the key and the value are treated as strings.

Exit Code or Exit Status a value, usually from 0 to 127, that represents the outcome of a command. 0 means the command succeeded. Any other value means it failed. Some commands document their exit codes so you can inspect the value to find out more details about why it failed. Used by Bash when running commands in a pipeline, using `&&`, or `||`.

File Descriptor An integer that UNIX interprets as an input or output stream.

Input Stream An abstraction that allows reading input. It is typically read in a loop until the stream is closed, which allows any amount of data to be read, since it doesn't have to fit into memory at the same time.

Output Stream An abstraction that allows sending output somewhere. It is typically used until whoever is writing to it closes it. This allows a potentially unlimited amount of data to be written.

Path A set of directories that will be searched for when you attempt to run a command. The path is a string where each directory is delimited by a colon. The directories are searched in order. You can inspect the path by examining the environment variable `PATH`, e.g. `echo $PATH`.

Process Something running on the computer, like your app, `ls`, `bash`, or a web server. A process is the lowest-level abstraction that you will deal with when using Bash or the command-line.

Shell An interpreter to interact with the operating system, typically initiated by a user logging into the system and executing commands.

Standard Error An output stream where command-line apps are expected to write error messages. This is file descriptor #2

Standard Input An input stream a command-line app can use to read input from the user or another command. This descriptor is #0.

Standard Output An output stream where command-line apps are expected to send whatever output they exist to output. Should not have error messages. This is file descriptor #1.

B.2 Symbol Soup

`/dev/null` A special file that discards everything sent to it. Used to hide output from scripts.

`>` e.g. `ls > file.txt` Redirect the *standard output* of a command into a file, overwriting that file.

`>>` e.g. `ls >> file.txt` Append the *standard output* of a command to the end of a file, creating it if needed.

`2>` e.g. `grep gem Gemfile 2> /dev/null` Redirect the *standard error* of a command into a file.

`2>&1` e.g. `grep gem Gemfile > /dev/null 2>&1` Combine the *standard error* of a command into its *standard output* and send them to wherever the > sent them (to `/dev/null` in this example)

`|` e.g. `echo ls | bash` Send the *standard output* of a command into the *standard input* of another command, thus creating a pipeline. Note that to cause the entire pipeline to fail if *any* command fails, you must `set -o pipefail` before running the pipelined commands.

`||` e.g. as in `bin/setup || echo 'failed'` If the command on the left of the `||` fails, run the command on the right. Otherwise, don't do that.

`&&` e.g. `bin/setup && echo 'OK'` If the command on the left of the `&&` fails, don't run the command on the right. Otherwise, run that command.

`;` e.g. `bin/setup ; echo 'No idea'` Separates commands, running each in order, regardless of the exit code of any command.

`&` e.g. `bin/run &` Runs a command in the background. When you do this, the shell will print a number inside brackets like so: `[3]`. You can then kill the process by running `kill %«number»` (e.g. `kill %3` in this example), or you can bring it back to the foreground via `fg %«number»` (e.g. `fg %3` in this example).

`#!` e.g. `#!/bin/bash` at the start of script. On the first line of a script, tells the operating system what program to use to interpret the remainder of the script.

`\` As seen in many code examples here, this allows you to split long lines onto multiple lines in the terminal.

`${VAR_NAME}` Access the value of a variable named `VAR_NAME` which could be in the UNIX environment or set as part of the script, *or* set on the command line.

`${0}` The name of the script currently being executed.

`${1}`, `${2}`, ... The arguments given to the script or function, with `${1}` being the first argument, `${2}` being the second and so on.

`'${VARNAME}'` or `'$VARNAME'` When used in a Bash script, the use of single quotes prevents `VARNAME` from being expanded into its value. The literal value inside the single quotes is used.

`"${VARNAME}"` or `"$VARNAME"` When used in a Bash script, the use of double quotes ensures that when `VARNAME`'s value is expanded, it is quoted and thus will not be misinterpreted as multiple arguments.

`"${@}"` A special form that expands to the Bash command's arguments list, with *each argument* properly quoted so that any command to which this is passed will interpret it the same way the Bash command did.

C

Protocols for Dev Environments

Your experience with the system is the sum of a remainder of an unbalanced equation inherent to our need to just get code into production quickly. Your support ticket is the eventuality of an anomaly, which despite my sincerest efforts, I have been unable to eliminate from what is otherwise a perfect system that works on my machine. While it remains a burden assiduously avoided, your bug report is not unexpected, and thus not beyond a measure of control. Which has led you, inexorably, to the JIRA backlog.

—*The System Architect's Guide to Customer Support*

In the book, we build the scripts `dx/build`, `dx/start`, `dx/stop`, and `dx/exec`. These scripts form a *protocol* that maintains the *Foundational Core* of where you work. Your *Workspace* should also conform to a similar protocol, ideally made up of similarly-designed scripts.

C.1 Foundational Core Protocol

`dx/build` Create any artifacts needed to establish the Foundational Core and use it to run your Workspace. In this book, `dx/build` creates a Docker image.

`dx/start` Start up the Foundational Core so it can be used. This should include anything needed for the Workspace, in addition to services it requires, like databases. In this book, this starts up the Docker container built by `dx/build` as well as all ancillary services, using Docker Compose.

`dx/stop` Stop the Foundational Core. In this book, this stops all Docker containers started by `dx/start`

`dx/exec «command»` Run a command in the context of the Foundational Core. In this book, this used `docker compose exec` to run commands inside the Docker container running the image built by `dx/build`

C.2 Workspace Protocol

The scripts here should be used if your chosen technology stack provides no other standardized way to perform the needed tasks. If your app's stack *does* provide command line mechanisms, but they are cumbersome or take lots of arguments, consider creating these scripts to wrap those complex commands. For example, instead of requiring your team to type `npm run server`, create `bin/dev` to wrap that call.

By adhering to this protocol, team workflow rarely has to change. If something about the app requires additional setup, that can be placed in `bin/setup`. If running the app requires a new way to configure a library, that can go into `bin/run`.

`bin/setup` Perform any app-specific setup, such as installed third-party libraries or seeding the dev database with data. It should assume that the Foundational Core is set up and running, however checking for this and providing an error message is always nice.

`bin/build` Build any artifacts needed to run the app in the dev environment. This would include compiling code that requires it, or bundling assets, if needed. This is a development task, so it should only do what is required based on the chosen tools for development. It should be designed to run exactly once and do whatever is necessary. `bin/dev` will handle running this in a loop to catch changes.

`bin/run` Run the app in development mode. Devs should be able to do `bin/setup && bin/build && bin/run` and begin interacting with the app.

`bin/dev` Run the app in development mode, re-building anything needed as code changes. This script exists to manage the "tweak and reload" workflow where you make code changes, then refresh your web browser to see your app updated with those changes. How this works largely depends on how your app is built. For example, a Ruby on Rails app only needs this to alias `bin/rails server`, since Rails includes auto-reloading.

`bin/ci` Run all tests and quality checks for your app. This would include security checks and other static analysis. Although your continuous integration system may require you to split up these tasks into a workflow, you should have this task configured to do everything needed. It can delegate to other scripts depending on your needs.

C.2.1 The World's Simplest `bin/dev` Script

Since you are running inside a UNIX-based Docker container, the following script can work as `bin/dev` for almost any app. You need to install NodeJS (which we learned how to do on page 37. Once you've done that, you'll need to install Chokidar CLI[1], which can be done in your Dockerfile like so:

```
RUN curl -fsSL https://deb.nodesource.com/setup_22.x -o node_setup.sh && \
    bash node_setup.sh && \
    apt-get install -y nodejs
```

[1]https://github.com/open-cli-tools/chokidar-cli

```
→ RUN npm install -g chokidar-cli
```

This will work even if your project doesn't use NodeJS (though your dev environment will need NodeJS installed). Here is `bin/dev`:

```
#!/usr/bin/env bash

set -e
set -o pipefail

trap killgroup SIGINT

killgroup() {
  echo "[ bin/dev ] Killing everything..."
  kill 0
}

SHELL=/bin/bash npx chokidar -p "src/**/*" -c "bin/build" &
bin/run &
wait
```

Replace `"src/**/*"` with wherever your app's source files are.

This uses some basic process management tools available on UNIX. The first few lines we've seen already. `trap` tells Bash that if a particular signal is received to run a command or function. In this case, it's *trapping* `SIGINT`, which is the name for the "interrupt" signal sent when you hit Ctrl-C. When that happens, this script will run the function `killgroup`.

Skipping `killgroup` for a second. Of the last three lines, the first runs `bin/build` from Chokidar. Chokidar will run the command given to `-c` whenever a file is changed anywhere in the path given to `-p`. Chokidar requires a `SHELL` environment variable to be set in order to work, and since it was installed with NodeJS, we must precede it with `npx`.

Note the trailing `&`, which will run Chokidar in the background. The script will proceed immediately to the next line where we run `bin/run` *also* in the background. The script proceeds to the last line, which is `wait`. `wait` waits for all processes launched in the background to complete.

This brings us back to `killgroup`. `bin/dev` will keep running until we hit Ctrl-C, at which point `trap` catches that signal and calls `killgroup`. `killgroup` echos what it is doing, then calls `kill 0`. `kill` stops a UNIX process by process ID. `0`, however, is a special value that means "stop all processes in the current process group", and a *process group* in this context contains all the processes we ran in the background.

Thus, `killgroup` will politely stop both Chokidar and `bin/run`. Nice!

A great lesson to takeaway from this is that even though UNIX can be extremely arcane, the needs of the average developer today were much the same as they were 10, 20, or even 30 years ago. And UNIX already has a solution for you.

D

Colophon or, The Chapter About Fonts

One does not simply choose a typeface. Its type foundries are guarded by more than just fussy designers. There is evil there that does not kern, and the Great Typesetter is ever watchful. It is a barren wasteland, riddled with leading and margins and ligatures, the very letterforms you examine are a poisonous baseline. Not even with Robert Bringhurst could you do this. It is folly.

—*Borimir*

The book is set in Utopia, with headings in ITC Avant Garde Gothic. Source code uses Inconsolata, while diagrams use Rufscript or Inconsolata. Epigraphs are in an italicized Utopia, using a slightly smaller size and leading. The cover is set in Anton, Buffalo, and Monsterrat Classic.

The text block of each page is based on the golden ratio with an attempt to provide enough width to accommodate all these ridiculously long command-line invocations and YAML source, without harming readability. Epigraphs are set in a width based on the golden ratio of the main text block's width. Hope you are feeling the symmetry and synergy.

The book was written primarily in Markdown (though a modified version that executes source code and command-line invocations, which you can read about it on my blog[1]). The Markdown was converted into either LaTeX or EPUB by Pandoc (and a `Makefile`, 'natch). Diagrams are created with Graphviz or Omnigraffle.

The majority of the original draft of this book was written while an interior brick wall of my house was being re-pointed. If you aren't familiar with this process, especially as it pertains to a row house built in the late 1800's, it requires many workers to pound the mortar out with hammers and chisels[2].

It creates a huge mess of rocks and dust and is very loud. To mix the mortar, the workers had to go in and out of my front door. The front door is not where I want

[1] https://www.naildrivin5.com/blog/2023/02/03/toolchain-for-building-programming-books.html

[2] Fun fact: pre-World-War-II masonry requires particular mortar to be used (in the United States, anyway). You can't just go get it easily from the hardware store and put it up yourself. If you used modern mortar, it will make the bricks crack and since they are holding up your house, you probably don't want that. Just an FYI for all you budding homeowners out there.

my cats (Carlos and Zoni) to be. However, as cats, they are honor-bound to be both curious and mischievous.

So, while drafting this book, I had to sit next to the front door to keep the cats from getting out, all while masons were pounding, pounding, and pounding on the wall of my house. Sometimes, figuring out why software won't install in Docker feels like this, so it's apt.

Made in United States
Orlando, FL
04 November 2026

90200512R00079